It was only a matter of time before a clever pub...... ...t there
is an audience for whom *Exile on Main Street* or *Electric Ladyland* are as
significant and worthy of study as *The Catcher in
the Rye* or *Middlemarch* ... The series ... is freewheeling and
eclectic, ranging from minute rock-geek analysis to idiosyncratic personal
celebration—*The New York Times Book Review*

Ideal for the rock geek who thinks liner notes
just aren't enough—*Rolling Stone*

One of the coolest publishing imprints on the planet—*Bookslut*

These are for the insane collectors out there who appreciate fantastic
design, well-executed thinking, and things that make your house look
cool. Each volume in this series takes a seminal album and breaks it
down in startling minutiae. We love these.
We are huge nerds—*Vice*

A brilliant series ... each one a work of real love—*NME* (UK)

Passionate, obsessive, and smart—*Nylon*

Religious tracts for the rock 'n' roll faithful—*Boldtype*

[A] consistently excellent series—*Uncut* (UK)

We ... aren't naive enough to think that we're your only
source for reading about music (but if we had our way ...
watch out). For those of you who really like to know everything
there is to know about an album, you'd do well to check
out Continuum's "33 1/3" series of books—*Pitchfork*

**For reviews of individual titles in the series, please visit
our blog at 333sound.com and our website at
http://www.bloomsbury.com/musicandsoundstudies**

Follow us on Twitter: @333books

Like us on Facebook: https://www.facebook.com/33.3books

For a complete list of books in this series, see the back of this book

For more information about the series, please visit our new blog:

www.333sound.com

Where you'll find:

– Author and artist interviews

– Author profiles

– News about the series

– How to submit a proposal to our open call

– Things we find amusing

Aja

Don Breithaupt

BLOOMSBURY ACADEMIC
NEW YORK · LONDON · OXFORD · NEW DELHI · SYDNEY

BLOOMSBURY ACADEMIC
Bloomsbury Publishing Inc
1385 Broadway, New York, NY 10018, USA
50 Bedford Square, London, WC1B 3DP, UK
29 Earlsfort Terrace, Dublin 2, Ireland

BLOOMSBURY, BLOOMSBURY ACADEMIC and the Diana logo are trademarks of
Bloomsbury Publishing Inc

First published in 2007 by the Continuum International Publishing Group Inc
Reprinted 2011
Reprinted by Bloomsbury Academic 2013, 2014, 2015, 2016, 2017 (twice), 2018,
2020, 2022, 2023 (twice)

© Don Breithaupt, 2007

Leonard, Paul, 1940—
Music of a thousand hammers : inside Habitat for Humanity / Paul
Leonard
p. cm
Includes index.
ISBN 0-8264-1842-2 (hardcover)
Habitat for Humanity International, Inc. 2. Leonard Paul 1940—
Low-income housing I. Title.
HV97.H32I.46 2006
363.5'83—dc22
2006002319
2007040095

ISBN: PB: 978-0-8264-2783-0
ePDF: 978-1-4411-1518-8
ePUB: 978-1-4411-8132-9

Series: 33 1/3, volume 46

Printed and bound in Great Britain

To find out more about our authors and books visit www.bloomsbury.com
and sign up for our newsletters.

Contents

Acknowledgments   vii
Preface   1

THIS ONE'S FOR REAL   3
Introduction

BLUEPRINT BLUE   8
Context

HEARD THIS ONE BEFORE   15
Influences

THIS IS THE DAY   23
Seventies

THROW OUT THE HARDWARE   28
Production

LIKE A ROMAN   32
Words

GET TO BENDIN' MY EAR   42
Harmony

BOOK OF NUMBERS   49
Sidemen

ANGULAR BANJOES   59
Guitar

TALK IT OUT TILL DAYLIGHT   65
Process

SOMEBODY ELSE'S FAVORITE SONG 69
FM (No Static at All)

YOU KNOW HOW TO HUSTLE   74
Fallout

THOSE OF MY KIND   82
Historical Moment

LAY DOWN THE LAW AND BREAK IT 90
Conclusion

Album Credits   100
Release Information / Chart History   105
Selected Covers   107
Glossary   109
Recommended Listening   122
Bibliography   129

Acknowledgments

First and foremost, my heartfelt thanks to Donald Fagen for agreeing to be interviewed for this book. He sat down with me at his Manhattan office last June, fielded a stack of nuts-and-bolts questions about the making of a thirty-year-old record, and was funny and forthcoming throughout (I think I got off to a good start by promising not to pose any hard-hitting, daily newspaper-style questions like "Which comes first, words or music?").

Additional thanks to: Brian Tomasini at Irving Azoff's office, who arranged the interview; Steve Khan, Lee Ritenour and Chuck Findley, who shed additional light on the *Aja* sessions and the composers' methods; Marc Jordan, who provided details of Fagen, Katz and Nichols's partici-pation in his debut album; series editor David Barker, who gave me invaluable direction from the beginning; Jay

Graydon, who supplied a raft of material about the final "Peg" guitar session; former *Metal Leg* editor and current Dan attaché Pete Fogel, who has done me more than a few favors over the years; and Steve Armour, whose friendship and insight are unwavering.

Finally, thanks as always to my long-suffering wife, Rikki (yes, Rikki), who, through no fault of her own, has the complete works of Steely Dan permanently lodged in her head.

Preface

The challenge was: don't gush. *It's your favorite album. You're going to write it a love letter and make a fool of yourself.*

I had already called *Aja* "the best record in the solar system" in print (in *Night Moves: Pop Music in the Late '70s*), so maybe, I told myself, the hyperbole was out of my system. Right. The hard part, as it turns out, wasn't squelching my enthusiasm: the hard part was properly explaining it. It's a well-worn adage that the easiest assignment in the world is reviewing something you can't stand—"Rod Stewart continues to have about him the air of squandered potential . . ."—and I've found that writing about something halfway likable is usually a snap too—"*Maroon* serves notice that Barenaked Ladies are tired of being your Yoko Ono and would like to be your John Lennon . . ."—but trying to explain why a particular recording implants itself in your DNA on first listening, well, that's tough. It feeds into other classic stumpers like: at what point does craft become art? And: does street-level popularity preclude artistic immortality? And (most importantly): who cares what I think?

It's worth noting that, for a band whose fans are on the literate side, Steely Dan have received comparatively little coverage in the book world. They are cited with regularity as innovators and jazz-rock alchemists in encyclopedias, but, apart from some glorified discographies and a 1994 biography for which the composers were not interviewed, Becker and Fagen are still awaiting the ink they deserve. I hope this slim volume, my very first epic record review, begins to address that shortfall.

A note regarding quotations: material from my own interviews with Donald Fagen and the other musicians appears in the text in present tense (i.e. "says Fagen"); material from books and periodicals appears in past tense and is directly attributed.

A note regarding technical language: I quickly determined while researching this book that I was not going to be able to write convincingly about Aja *without delving into its musical and technical underpinnings (Steely Dan aren't a garage band). Aware that some readers will find the terminology within occasionally baffling, I have included in the appendices a detailed glossary.*

THIS ONE'S FOR REAL
Introduction

Aja was the album that made Steely Dan a commercial force on the order of contemporaries like Fleetwood Mac and the Eagles. A multiplatinum Grammy-winner, it lingered on the *Billboard* charts for more than a year and spawned three hit singles. Odd, then, that it was conceived as the apotheosis of its creators' anti-rock, anti-band, anti-glamour aesthetic. Populated only by Walter Becker, Donald Fagen and thirty-five of their closest friends—many of them jazz musicians —*Aja* served up modified prewar song forms, mixed meters and extended solos to a generation whose idea of pop daring was Paul letting Linda sing lead once in a while. And, impossibly, it sold.

Becker and Fagen, always the nucleus of Steely Dan and now its sole survivors, regarded their success dispassionately. If *Aja* did big business, there would be a big budget for its successor; everything else was incidental. "The main thing was that they would let us keep making records," says Fagen. "We were mainly concerned with the quality. While we were making the records, we thought they were all good. Then, after a while, we didn't like them anymore for various reasons, and we'd say, 'Well, we have to make a better one now.' We weren't worried about sales; we were just worried that if we didn't have sales that equaled the first one, they wouldn't give us a budget." The two composers had turned in their rock star credentials after retiring from the road in 1974, and, like the Beatles after *Revolver*, had retreated to the studio and locked the insulated door behind them. *Aja* was their latest salvo. As the accolades rolled in—*Newsweek* had recently dubbed them "the best American rock group of the seventies"—Becker and Fagen were already back in the lab crafting the stand-alone, album rock–spoofing single "FM (No Static at All)."

Even when *Aja*'s songs clocked in at under six minutes, they eschewed pop formalism in favor of pan-generic mischief: the swampy R&B groove of "Josie" became a platform for modal interpolations out of the postbop songbook; the hypnotic lope of the mini-*Odyssey* "Home at Last" was interrupted by a synthesized big band interlude; "I Got the News" littered its serene major-sixth vamp with angular piano figures that recalled Thelonius Monk. *Aja*'s gatefold sleeve even featured Blue Note Records–style liner notes.

And then there were the lyrics. The suicidal loner, the

chatty lecher and the drug-addled princess had antecedents in the Dan canon, but this time Becker and Fagen's dark visions came off as even more sinister by virtue of their sparkling surroundings. Like Randy Newman, another west-coast ironist who regularly availed himself of LA's A-list session players, Steely Dan were fascinated by—indeed, often empathized with—characters on the fringes of society. Newman's "In Germany Before the War" (from *Little Criminals*, released the same year as *Aja*) cloaked a killer in lush strings and tinkling piano. Steely Dan's smoldering, sax-drenched "Deacon Blues" made dying drunk in a post-mid-night car wreck sound like a heroic consummation devoutly to be wish'd.

Throughout, the usual Steely Dan dualities were in play. All seven of the new narratives were told in first person, but they kept listeners at an almost palpable distance—longer than arm's length, let's say, but generally within the 212 or 213 area codes. Becker and Fagen remained a rock band in the public consciousness, but functioned behind the scenes more like a countercultural Bacharach/David. They were clearly in love with late-fifties jazz, whose hallmark was spontaneity, but often edited their celebrated soloists' performances together phrase by phrase. Their heroes were improvisers, Beat poets and hard-grooving soul stars, but their work was possessed of a hi-tech spit polish that belied their tastes. Indeed, each record seemed more worked out than the previous one, even down to the sequencing of songs: "Occasionally we would have a tune that we knew we wanted to start with, or be the second, or be at the end, so we placed those," says Fagen. "Sometimes a tune would come out really strong and we'd say, 'Well, we have to start with this now.' There were times when, during the course of the record, we decided that a certain song had to follow a certain other song, in which case we'd actually change the end of one of them if we didn't like the transition, the key."

Still, for those in its spell, Steely Dan's music has a free-wheeling rush to it, a sense of exhilaration that comes at least in part from the sense that boundaries are being tested, rules of pop conduct are being subverted—not subverted Velvet Underground–style, where craft is cast aside in favor of studied simplicity, but subverted by craft itself. When the cultural bar has been lowered to the point of absurdity, the only revenge worthy of the name comes from reestablishing standards lost to laziness and expediency. It's what the Beatles did at the end of the Frankie Avalon era. An album like *Aja* matters not just because it contributes to civilization a handful of date-stamped audio treasures, but because it puts into sharp relief the dreck that surrounds it. How else to know the true banality of "Come Sail Away," "Hot Legs" and "Three Times a Lady" (all of which shared chart space with songs from *Aja*)?

The notion of giving a hero's welcome to two book-wormish jazz aficionados utterly unconcerned with getting their live ya-ya's out may not appeal to critics who subscribe to the "noble savage" theory of rock and roll, but inspiration isn't bestowed on the basis of methodology, locale or educational background. To the muses, Manhattan is as good as Memphis, and Bard College, Becker and Fagen's liberal-arts alma mater, is as good as the school of hard knocks. If we're lucky, the twentieth century's best popular art will outlive that hackneyed (if not racist) debate. Authenticity comes from the darnedest places.

BLUEPRINT BLUE
Context

Creatio ex nihilo, making something out of nothing, is rare in popular music. Yes, Miles Davis rolled out of bed on the morning of March 2, 1959, and reinvented jazz (*Kind of Blue*), and Marvin Gaye erased ten years of Motown finishing school over a few weeks in early 1971 (*What's Going On*), but most contemporary recordings represent baby steps, incremental progress along an artistic continuum. This is true even of albums routinely regarded as landmarks. Freed from its extraordinary historical moment, *Sgt. Pepper's Lonely Hearts Club Band* sounds like what it is: the album after *Revolver*. *Sticky Fingers* is the main tributary of *Exile on Main Street*, which empties into *Goats Head Soup*.

All of which is to say that 1977's *Aja*, the album most often cited by critics and devotees as Steely Dan's crowning achievement, is demonstrably a melodic/harmonic/rhythmic cousin of its predecessors (in particular *The Royal Scam* and *Katy Lied*) and a template for its immediate successors (*Gaucho* and Donald Fagen's *The Nightfly*). This is partly a function of the rapid-fire creativity dictated by commercial record deals in the seventies. Since their 1972 debut, *Can't Buy a Thrill*, Steely Dan had maintained a record-a-year pace, hectic by today's standards but not unusual in the day: over the same six-year period, Elton John, Stevie Wonder, Bob Marley, David Bowie, Joni Mitchell, James Taylor, Neil Young, Al Green, Aretha Franklin, Eric Clapton and all four ex-Beatles had maintained similarly dense recording schedules. Jumping back into the studio while your previous record was still being mined for singles made for releases that were often more like chapters of one long book than freestanding works.

"We started to get it right around *Katy Lied* and *The Royal Scam*," says Donald Fagen of the mid-seventies albums that saw Steely Dan shed most of their original roster. "That's when it started to get its own sound." Those records—the band's fourth and fifth—contain the seeds of *Aja*, not just in their songwriters-plus-sidemen approach, but in specific instrumentation, melodic fragments, harmonic concepts and rhythmic figures that bore repeating.

Katy Lied (1975) was a mission statement for the new, stay-at-home Dan. With explicit ties to blues, jazz and funk, it signaled Becker and Fagen's disinclination to concoct another "Rikki Don't Lose That Number," the hit that had vaulted the previous year's *Pretzel Logic* into the *Billboard* Top 10. It saw Steely Dan compositionally embracing the sixth (or submediant) scale degree, a note whose stock had been falling steadily in the pop world roughly since 1964, when Sam Cooke, one of its last champions, was murdered in Los Angeles. In the swing era, the sixth had been used frequently in popular melodies (see Robins and Shavers's "Undecided" or Count Basie's "Jumpin' at the Woodside"), even as a point of resolution, but by 1975 it was considered corny, especially in rock circles. This was partly a result of the demise of the I^6 chord; in rock, the default chord for the tonic position was a garden-variety major triad. Becker and Fagen had introduced the sixth into the Dan vocabulary, both as an era-appropriate bass note and prominent melody note, with 1974's "Parker's Band," their tribute to bebop progenitor Charlie Parker. On *Katy Lied,* they ran with it: the verse vamp of "Bad Sneakers" is built on an A^6 chord; the chorus of "Bad Sneakers" begins with a melodic sixth (A in the new key of C); the sixth colors the chorus-concluding tutti figure of "Your Gold Teeth II"; and "Chain Lightning," an altered twelve-bar blues about the seductive power of fascism, includes prominent sixths in its bassline, harmony and melody (it's built on the same thirteenth-chord cliché as Miles Davis's "Freddie Freeloader"). Retro strokes like these were symptomatic of the duo's increasing comfort level with their jazz roots, and may not have been premeditated: as Fagen points out, "There wasn't that much planning. I can't think of a moment when we did anything that was other than intuitive." Either way, by the time of *Aja*, the sixth was a core Steely Dan compositional element, present in the exposed basslines of "Black Cow" and "I Got the News," the instrumental hook of "Peg" and, via Miles once again, in the guitar/Rhodes comping figure in "Black Cow." (For post-*Aja* sixth content, look to "My Rival," "Time Out of Mind" and "New Frontier.")

Katy Lied was also the album on which Becker and Fagen decided to get specific about the people, places and things surrounding their characters. On "Turn That Heartbeat Over Again," from *Can't Buy a Thrill* (1972), it had seemed sufficient for the narrator to address Sam the bartender thus:

> My poison's named
> You know my brand

By 1975, Steely Dan were ready to let us know Lucy's drink of choice was "Coke and rum" ("Daddy Don't Live in That New York City No More"), and to make "piña colada" part of a key repeated line ("Bad Sneakers"). On *The Royal Scam* (1976), Babs drank "the zombie from the cocoa shell" ("Haitian Divorce"). In addition to having a song named for a rootbeer float ("Black Cow"), *Aja* mentioned Scotch whiskey ("Deacon Blues") and retsina, an ancient variety of Greek wine flavored with pine resin ("Home at Last").

Things got even more specific on "FM (No Static at All)" (grapefruit wine), *Gaucho* (Cuervo Gold, cherry wine and kirschwasser, a black cherry liqueur) and *The Nightfly* ("Pour me a Cuban Breeze"). *Now* your poison's named.

Drinking establishments, too, began to show up with increasing frequency, starting on *The Royal Scam*: the crumbling, futuristic landscape of "Sign in Stranger" included a fictional club called the Café D'Escargot; *Aja*'s "Black Cow" was set in Rudy's; *Gaucho*'s "My Rival" name-checked Anthony's. Late-model Dan records have taken up the gauntlet, with "the Smokehouse in the Sand" and "Club Hi Ho" among the landmarks on Fagen's *Kamakiriad* (1993) and "the bar at Joey's" part of the virtual reality in "Green Book," a dark, funky gem from *Everything Must Go* (2003). A minor thread of religious imagery that began on *Katy Lied* ("The Archbishop's gonna sanctify me," "halfway crucified") continued on *The Royal Scam* ("Be born again," "I wanna be your holy man," "Did you feel like Jesus?") and *Aja* ("prays like a Roman"), and the Asian theme extant in the Dan repertoire as early as 1973's *Countdown to Ecstasy*—a Bodhisattva is a magnanimous Buddhist—showed up in *Aja*'s title track ("Chinese music under banyan trees"), *Gaucho*'s "Time Out of Mind" (Lhasa, the Tibetan home of the Dalai Lama) and *The Nightfly*'s "Green Flower Street" ("mandarin plum"). *Pretzel Logic* (1974) marked the start of Becker and Fagen's cinematic bent: "With a Gun" and the title track reference "western movies" and "the movie show" respectively. The motif gained momentum over the next few albums, with *Katy Lied*'s "Everyone's Gone to the Movies," *The Royal Scam*'s "Haitian Divorce"—

> Now we dolly back
> Now we fade to black

—and *Aja*'s "Peg." *Gaucho*'s "Glamour Profession" actually begins like a screenplay—6:05, OUTSIDE THE STADIUM—and includes the phrase "celluloid bikers" (think Dennis Hopper's *Easy Rider* or even Kenneth Anger's *Scorpio Rising*).

The Royal Scam, Steely Dan's so-called "guitar album," is even more clearly a cousin of *Aja*. It introduced instrumental textures—the title track's muted trumpet breaks, the clavinet comping in "Kid Charlemagne," Larry Carlton's soaring guitar leads—that would become staples on *Aja* and beyond. It cemented jazz-derived non-triadic chord voicings—open fourths in the verses of "Don't Take Me Alive" and "Green Earrings," maj^9-no-third stacks in "The Caves of Altamira" (F#/B, E/A, C#/F#) and "Don't Take Me Alive" (Bb/Eb, C/F, D/G)—as Becker and Fagen's permanent replacement for standard pop harmony, clearing the way for the stark, contemporary colors of "Josie" and "I Got the News." It also established new formal conceits, like the tension/release pattern of the title track's verses: two bars of dense, shifting harmony with vocal followed by a comparatively simple vamp, over and over. "I Got the

News" and *Gaucho*'s "Third World Man" reused the pattern.

Aja in turn created context for *Gaucho* (1980) and *The Nightfly* (1982). If "Peg" was a nod to disco, *Gaucho*'s "Glamour Profession" was an outright endorsement (Fagen confessed at the time to a fondness for Dr. Buzzard's Original "Savannah" Band). The instrumental break in "Home at Last" marked the first appearance of the sinewy, harmonica-like lead that would become Donald Fagen's signature synthesizer sound on "Hey Nineteen" and "I.G.Y. (What a Beautiful World)." Bernard Purdie, the legendary drummer who had played on classic soul sides like Aretha Franklin's "Rock Steady" and James Brown's "Ain't That a Groove," used his trademark half-time shuffle on "Home at Last," and the lightly swinging, ghost stroke–peppered groove became the rhythmic architecture for "Babylon Sisters" and the 1988 one-off "Century's End."

Aja is to *The Royal Scam* and *Gaucho* as Stevie Wonder's *Innervisions* is to *Talking Book* and *Fulfillingness' First Finale*: it represents one signpost on a pathway of extraordinary, genre-bending creativity, and can be distinguished stylistically from its immediate musical neighbors only through careful analysis. That doesn't mean it isn't the magnum opus it's cracked up to be—even its authors have copped to its greatness by statistically over-representing it in their live repertoire since returning to touring in 1993—just that it's part of a continuum. Masterpieces don't come out of thin air. Not lately, anyway.

HEARD THIS ONE BEFORE
Influences

In its slightly conflicted original review of *Aja*, *Rolling Stone* called Steely Dan "the only group around with no conceptual antecedent from the '60s." (*Rolling Stone* was, at the time, the only magazine around with no conceptual antecedent from anything *but* the sixties.) Reviewer Michael Duffy's point was that Becker and Fagen had consistently reached into the pre-rock canon for inspiration, which was true, but, as Donald Fagen has pointed out, Steely Dan's influences also included baby boomer favorites like Bob Dylan, the Band, Ray Charles, Frank Zappa, Carole King, Bacharach/David, Leiber/Stoller and, yes, the Beatles: "The main thing we got from the Beatles was the idea that each album should be a gift. You shouldn't take it lightly. I remember in the sixties, starting with *Rubber Soul*, they'd come out with an album, and it always seemed like they'd worked on it really hard so it wouldn't be disappointing." So, while their contemporaries were making off with entire Lennon/McCartney melodies and turns of phrase, Steely Dan stole the Beatles' work ethic. Never was their hang-the-cost devotion more apparent than during the year-plus *Aja* sessions (five months on mixes alone): ABC had to reschedule the album's release date three times.

Over and above the oft-cited Dylanesque inflections in Fagen's singing—compare "Positively 4th Street" and "Barrytown," especially the lines "You see me on the street" and "If they see you on the street"—the sixties' lyricist laureate also widened the Dan's thematic purview. "Without Bob Dylan, no one could do anything," says Fagen. "I'm not saying he was terribly conscious of the things he did, but that's the way it turned out. You know, just an idea that seems simple now, like: you can write a song about anything. No one had ever thought of that before. And can you write a whole album about that anything, and still have some variety? Dylan never did a concept album, and yet, what is *Highway 61 Revisited* or *Blonde on Blonde*?" *Aja*'s scenarios, none of them love songs, are all verifiably post-Dylan: "Aja" ain't "Bali Hai," "Peg" ain't "You Oughta Be in Pictures," "Josie" ain't "Let's Have a Party."

By and large, though, the legend is true: Becker and Fagen were ardent devotees of jazz, blues and the Great American Songbook, and made it their business to reintroduce these ingredients into mainstream pop. In blues, they found the genetic strand that links jazz, rock and soul. "Blues is the most important ingredient of pop music," Fagen told sometime fellow traveler Warren Bernhardt in Homespun Video's excellent *Concepts for Jazz/Rock Piano* (1993). "That's what really gives it the soul and the forward motion. Just starting with a regular blues structure is the way a lot of [our] songs were written . . . taking that and expanding it either harmonically or changing the structure, so you have a basic blues feeling to it, but you end up with a song that's more complex." Becker and Fagen had tinkered with the blues before—"Bodhisattva" (1973), "Pretzel Logic" (1974), "Chain Lightning" (1975) are all blues forms whose devious non-diatonic chords constitute actual key changes—but never as on *Aja*. The architecture of the blues is nothing less than the underpinning of the album's entire second side.

The animus behind the verses in "Peg" is this: for each of the standard three chords of a twelve-bar blues (tonic, subdominant and dominant), substitute a plagal cadence, the familiar "Amen" IV-to-I sound. In the key of G Major, this means the I chords in the progression (bars 1, 2, 3, 4, 7, 8, 11 and 12) consist of a C to a G, or IV-of-I to I, the IV chords in the progression (bars 5, 6 and 10) consist of an F to a C, or IV-of-IV to IV, and the V chord in the progression (bar 9) consists of a G to a D, or IV-of-V to V. Because the resolution chord in each pair sounds mid-bar, the cadences are feminine, meaning they don't resolve strongly on downbeats. So far, the effect is novel, but not shocking: even the F chord, technically outside the key of G, is idiomatically at home in a blues setting. But Becker and Fagen push the notion one step further by adding major sevenths to the supplementary chords (B to the C, E to the F, F# to the G), making the overall color of the progression insistently major. This amounts to deconstruction of the most delicious kind: throughout "Peg," the Ionian cheer of the harmony is at odds with the moodiness implied by the blues structure. It's the main reason so many crack guitarists had trouble soloing on the tune. (Interestingly, the verse progression that emerged from the tracking date was not quite what Fagen had in mind: "I'd used those two chords before, sort of a IV-to-III progression, and the idea was to make a blues using only those two chords, without hitting a I chord. There really wasn't a I chord in it until [bassist] Chuck Rainey started playing the tune, and he decided to play the tonic in his part. It sounded good, so it didn't really bother me that it wasn't what was theoretically intended.")

"Home at Last" is not technically a blues, but leaves a bluesy impression by virtue of its rolling shuffle, the IVm-to-Im cadence at the top of the chorus, and Larry Carlton's clean-Strat, Chicago Blues–style comping figure. "I Got the News" has an oddball form that defies easy definition, but it cleaves to the blues tradition by virtue of its hook: just as Fagen sings the line "I got the news," the harmony jumps from a I^7 to a IV^7 and back again, and, to western ears, that combination says "blues," almost irrespective of context. "Josie," with its stark open fifths and lyric-driven rhythm, gets its inspiration from the Delta blues, but colors its verse with exotic open chords derived from the parallel Phrygian scale, even as the vocal melody remains basically minor-pentatonic—blue, for lack of a better word. (Steely Dan's blues-warping ways have continued into the twenty-first century: "What a Shame About Me," "Cousin Dupree," "Godwhacker" and "The Last Mall," from *Two Against Nature* and *Everything Must Go*, are all modified blues progressions. For *Aja*-era examples by other artists, start with Stevie Wonder's mid-seventies catalog, paying special attention to "Superstition," "Living for the City," "Higher Ground" and "Have a Talk with God," and continue through David Bowie's "Fame," Van Morrison's "Blue Money" and Paul Simon's "One Man's Ceiling Is Another Man's Floor.")

It was largely via their shared love of jazz that Becker and Fagen bonded while attending Bard College, up the Hudson from New York City, together in 1967 and 1968. Fagen had grown up listening to his mother singing standards around the house; Becker had taken up the guitar during adolescence. Both—Fagen in suburban New Jersey, Becker in Queens—had been aided and abetted in their jazz self-education by the robust New York jazz radio scene of the fifties and early sixties. With multiple streams of current jazz being spun and elucidated by local on-air greats Symphony Sid, Ed Beach and especially *Jazz Unlimited* host Mort Fega, who championed many a future Dan influence, it was almost unnecessary for young Donald and Walter to patronize the jazz clubs in Manhattan (although they did that too: Fagen told *Melody Maker* one trip into town to hear Charles Mingus was like "a visitation from another universe").

Vestiges of these formative experiences can be found throughout *Aja*. In addition to the improvised solos (minimum one per song, usually more) and impossibly laid-back grooves, there are the sly horn arrangements, lapping away in stacked fourths or tight clusters behind Fagen's voice. "I liked Gil Evans," says Fagen. "He didn't write too high very often. For the horns, Walter and I would use the phrase that was often applied to Miles Davis, which was 'middle register brooding.' It was a little joke." "Aja's" tranquil vocal melody opens with a stepwise fragment centered around the seventh degree of the scale—in B Major, the phrase ("Up on the hill . . . ") is A#, B, A#, G#—a decidedly old-fashioned place to start. Even in an eight-minute, harmonically wayward, contemporary piece, then, Becker and Fagen remained rooted in American songcraft: standards with similar openings include "Manhattan" (Rodgers/Hart, 1925), "The Song Is You" (Kern/Hammerstein, 1932), "Pennies from Heaven" (Johnston/Burke, 1936), "In the Still of the Night" (Porter, 1937) and "Stella by Starlight" (Young/ Washington, 1946).

Aja is brimming with jazz chord changes, so much so

that to itemize just a few risks understating the matter. However, by way of example, consider the climactic III-VI-II-V of "Peg's" chorus, the vamp-busting moment in "Black Cow" when an $A^{7(b9b13)}$ leads to a Dm^{11}, and the $Gb^{7(b5)}$ in bar 7 of the chorus of "Deacon Blues." All these colors enrich what might otherwise have been stock pop moments; that $Gb^{7(b5)}$ could just as easily have been omitted in order to land the IV chord ($Fmaj^7$) on a downbeat. Add to the list of jazz content the lyric to "Deacon Blues," whose key location is a smoky club wherein our hero plans to face down his demons, horn in hand ("stand" in this excerpt meaning both "final effort" and "bandstand"):

> I take one last drag
> As I approach the stand

Like most of their colleagues, Steely Dan wore their influences on their sleeve. It's just that so many of their influences came from the years before the great divide, before the onset of rock and roll. Colors that seemed to Becker and Fagen to be part of the very fabric of popular music sounded, to many second- and third-generation rock fans, entirely alien. Forget Louis Jordan, Chuck Berry and Fats Domino; by 1977, most rock bands weren't reaching back much further than mid-period Beatles. The perception was, and is, that Steely Dan insisted on challenging listeners just for the mischievous fun of it, and it's true they never dumbed anything down. But they were just building new objects out of the materials lying around in their larger-than-average artistic backyard. As Lee Ritenour says, "They were the singer-songwriters who loved jazz." They never figured out why that was such an affront.

THIS IS THE DAY
Seventies

Conventional wisdom tells us the artists that made up the California scene of the seventies were of a piece, as though Warren Zevon's methods were Ry Cooder's, as though it could be anything but geographical accident that Lowell George and Al Jarreau were making records in the same city. Reductionist malarkey! California pop was as varied and finally précis-proof as the era-shattering commotion that followed it. Shared colleagues (Rick Marotta, Don Grolnick, Sherlie Matthews) aside, Steely Dan had about as much in common with Linda Ronstadt as Elvis Costello had with Bananarama.

West Coast music was commonly associated with the earnest, first-person folk rock of Jackson Browne, but the airing out of emotional laundry interested Steely Dan not at all: Donald Fagen approvingly cited a *New York Times* interview in which Randy Newman had decried the then-current mania for "personal" songs. Neither Becker nor Fagen was the implied "I" in their lyrics, and their penchant for irony meant nothing could be taken at face value. When Steely Dan told you to how to have fun, fun, fun (see "Everyone's Gone to the Movies"), they weren't driving you to the beach in Brian Wilson's 409—they were setting you up with the neighborhood whack job for an unchaperoned afternoon watching Super-8 porn. Los Angeles, the "dude ranch above the sea," was all about everlasting summer; Steely Dan, the palest troubadours in the San Fernando Valley, were all about how it feels when it's fading fast.

If Becker and Fagen were philosophically out of step with their fellow Los Angelenos, they were hardly immune to the culture at large. "We liked Stevie Wonder, of course," says Fagen. "You know who I thought were going to do something really nice? Those two guys called Seals & Crofts. They had a very nice way of integrating jazz into their tunes. And I really liked Dan Hicks and His Hot Licks, and Stuff [Steve Gadd, Eric Gale, Richard Tee and company] in New York. John Sebastian was a great musician. I was influenced by the Lovin' Spoonful a lot, especially as far as singing goes. I really dig John's phrasing and the way he used to work his way around rhythmically. I liked Herbie Hancock's stuff. I thought *Head Hunters* was kind of repetitive—those grooves would just go on—but he really knew how to get a nice sound. And I loved the drummers: Harvey Mason, all those guys who played with Herbie. I liked his guitarists, too, guys out in LA like Wah Wah Watson." When Fagen was tapped as a guest for the BBC's long-running *Desert Island Discs* radio show in 1990, he delineated his seventies tastes with a decade's perspective, spinning tracks obviously Dan-compatible (Rickie Lee Jones's "Chuck E's in Love," the Grateful Dead's "Shakedown Street," War's "Low Rider") and not (Elton John's "Bennie and the Jets," Neil Young's "Heart of Gold," John Lennon's "Instant Karma").

Even when something recognizably current infiltrated one of their records—*Aja* had the occasional Crusaders-like stretch—Steely Dan were finally a set of one. They were often said to represent some kind of fusion of jazz and rock, but were not a fusion group in the sense that, say, Return to Forever was. "I didn't follow that debate, to tell you the truth," says Fagen. "Most of the things that were called jazz rock that I was familiar with were pretty boring. I remember Jeremy [Steig] and the Satyrs, a jammy kind of group that was really boring. And *Bitches Brew* was essentially just a big trash-out for Miles. I haven't really changed my mind about that. I liked *In a Silent Way*, but *Bitches Brew* just sounded kind of funny. It would have made a good soundtrack for a Fat Albert cartoon—but not as good as the Herbie Hancock one they actually had! To me it was just silly, and out of tune, and bad. I couldn't listen to it. It sounded like [Davis] was shooting for a funk record, and just picked the wrong guys. They didn't understand how to play funk. They weren't steady enough. You know what I kind of liked? The Don Ellis big band. It was popular in New York. He had a quarter-tone trumpet, and there was this nice boogalooy big band chart they used to play on the jazz stations. But there wasn't that much happening." The jazz-rock tag, like other classifications, was used by journalists because it was convenient. Steely Dan were part of the California scene, but only because they happened to be there, not because they shared any particular Left Coaster's artistic aims (with the possible exception of Randy Newman). As future *New York Times* critic Jon Pareles observed in *Crawdaddy!* at the time, they were "so far removed from any competition that perhaps their only amusement [came] from outdoing themselves."

The *Village Voice*'s 1977 "Pazz & Jop" poll found *Aja* (number 5) surrounded by numerous punk and punk-related albums: the Sex Pistols' *Never Mind the Bollocks, Here's the Sex Pistols*, Elvis Costello's *My Aim Is True*, Graham Parker & the Rumour's *Stick to Me* and the Jam's *In the City* from London; Television's *Marquee Moon*, Talking Heads' *Talking Heads: 77*, Mink DeVille's eponymous debut and the Ramones' *Rocket to Russia* from New York. This served not to so much to contextualize *Aja* as to isolate it. Rock stringers of the day were falling all over themselves to reward dyspeptic do-it-yourself record makers for whom slickness was the cardinal sin; surely Becker and Fagen were the only auteurs in radioland scoring critical points with major ninth chords and hired sidemen.

The eighties would see facile irony become the preferred philosophical stance of the English-speaking world. And MIDI, the digital protocol that enabled drum machines and synthesizers to communicate with their streaky-haired operators and each other, would put mathematical near-perfection within easy reach of some truly depressing opportunists (if you're a Flock of Seagulls fan, you bought the wrong book). So perhaps it makes sense that Becker and Fagen hibernated, virtually museless, for much of the Reagan era. Needing to press, to insist on supranatural results against all odds, to purvey ambiguity in an era of bald sincerity, was the whole game. Once the kind of smart-alecky prattle and hum typified by Madonna's "Material Girl" and Duran Duran's "The Reflex" became pop's stock-in-trade, Steely Dan no longer had their rarefied domain to themselves. Panderers had co-opted their mission, at least a goofball version of it. Becker and Fagen would lie in wait until the junk bond decade was over.

THROW OUT THE HARDWARE
Production

Despite several nominations, *Aja*'s only Grammy award was for engineering, which is a bit like giving the ceiling of the Sistine Chapel a trophy for "best matte finish." Yes, the sound of Steely Dan records is of measurable importance to fans and audiophiles alike—for years, *Aja* was the preferred nonclassical demo disc of high-end stereo shops—but it's not really part of the works themselves, right? Not so fast. If we allow that Becker and Fagen's legendary patience in the pursuit of excellence encompasses not just composition, but in-studio matters, then it also encompasses clarity, balance, stereo image, dynamic range and overall fidelity. To paraphrase Yeats, how can we know the overdubber from the overdub?

The tension between Steely Dan's dystopic slices of life and their sleek delivery system is integral to the composers' postmodern method. Becker and Fagen's best work often hinges on upbeat form fighting downbeat content. The apocalyptic scenarios in "The Last Mall" (2003), "Black Friday" (1975) and "King of the World" (1973), for example, are offset by indelible hooks, impeccably constructed grooves, and, in the case of the last song, a monophonic synthesizer lead that speaks to midcentury fantasies of technological progress. Would they be less effective if cast in darker hues, without the crisp, airtight production? Look no further than ponderous eighties antinuclear tracts like Heaven 17's "Let's All Make a Bomb," the Fixx's "Red Skies" and Violent Femmes' "Hallowed Ground" for a definitive *yes*. It's all well and gloomy to hear civilization is circling the drain, but when the accompanying audio suggests the future is rosy, the bad news is doubly startling.

The stakes are lower in *Aja*'s stories—addiction, jealousy and ennui stand in for Armageddon—but the contrast is even sharper. Nothing, certainly nothing in the rock realm, has ever sounded quite as microscopically detailed or sonically sure of itself as Steely Dan's sixth album; in such a pristine soundscape, it's easy to miss things like the conquering hero's self-doubt in "Home at Last" and the impending danger behind the upscale tryst in "I Got the News." The burned-out beloved in "Black Cow" may be facedown on the counter at Rudy's Bar & Grill, but her story is being told with such sparkling nonchalance, it's initially hard to feel the words' Sisyphean angst. Such ambiguity isn't the only pathway to greatness—Tom Waits's debauched "Union Square" (1985) sounds so magnificently scuzzy, you can almost smell the urine stench blowing up the stairs at the 14th Street Station—but it's integral to the Dan worldview.

It's telling that Steely Dan had lost somewhere between five and ten band members (depending on your definition of band membership) in the years leading up to *Aja*, but had never tampered with their original production/engineering tandem of Gary Katz, who had helped secure their deal with ABC-Dunhill, and Roger Nichols, who shared his 1978 engineering Grammy with Elliot Scheiner, Bill Schnee and Al Schmidt. The implication is clear: it was more important for Becker and Fagen to surround themselves with people who shared their technical vision than it was to have a permanent team of players and singers. (Not that they were always of one mind: "Walter, Elliott and Roger used to fuss with the drums to the point where I had to walk out of the room," says Fagen.)

The list of contemporary musicians for whom production values assume thematic importance is a short one. Studio hermits like Todd Rundgren, Prince and Lewis Taylor achieve a sometimes claustrophobic consistency of tone via compulsive multitracking. Radiohead strew their post-progrock songs with electronic debris that is a literal expression of their fragmented, wired characters. Fountains of Wayne marshal all the surface elements of seventies power pop and corporate rock even as they skewer the suburbs, where those styles flourished. And Steely Dan's painstaking soundcraft is more than neurotic indulgence: it's the mechanism by which we are allowed to watch their sublime creations deconstruct themselves.

LIKE A ROMAN
Words

Pressed by Joseph Gelmis in 1969 for a literal explanation of
his latest masterpiece, *2001: A Space Odyssey*, Stanley Kubrick
pointed out "you don't need written instructions by the
composer" when confronted with "a fine piece of music."
Accordingly, Steely Dan have always been loath to shed light
on their slightly cryptic lyrics. Interviewers who dare to ask
the taciturn duo for details about the real-life Rikki, Katy,
Peg or Josie, for example, are invariably denied (and sometimes humiliated). When it strives for mere verisimilitude,
rock criticism is akin to autopsy.

For at least a year after *Aja*'s release, everyone's favorite
Steely Dan question was "Who or *what* is 'Aja'?" Research
yields interesting but finally irrelevant answers: a West
African tribe; a mythical Hindu king; a Yoruban forest spirit; a Nilo-Saharan language; the *American Journal of Archeology*.

Fagen has said the title came from a schoolmate whose soldier brother returned from Korea newly wedded to a woman named Aja (spelling uncertain), but in the title song the word seems to be shorthand for peace, exotica, the alluring other, even death. The lyrics paint Aja as a nonspecific, though certainly eastern, place far from the worlds of celebrity, commerce, even linear time—a place in which a troubled spirit might find solace.

Like Joni Mitchell's *Hejira* (1976), *Aja* is an album about flux and wanderlust. Its hapless adventurers seek relief from romantic detachment ("Black Cow," "I Got the News," "Peg"), tedium ("Aja"), exile ("Home at Last") and inertia ("Deacon Blues," "Josie"), relief from a peculiarly modern species of disquiet whose name just might be "Los Angeles." Having lived in California for the better part of a decade, Becker and Fagen were craving their gritty East Coast home turf. *Aja*'s lyrics contain not only specific New York locations—Rudy's Bar & Grill, Greene Street, Broadway—but Runyonesque characters that in the composers' minds must have seemed specifically Gotham. (Ironically, Becker and Fagen would make their Chandleresque LA album, *Gaucho*, only after returning to NYC in the late seventies.)

Aja was rendered in Steely Dan's distinctive urban argot, and was possessed of a level of detail and craft that had all but disappeared in popular song since the deaths of Cole Porter, Frank Loesser and Dorothy Fields. In "Black Cow," an ABCBBDD rhyme scheme is strictly observed in all four verse stanzas, and vowel sounds are meticulously matched inside lines:

> You were *high*
> It was a *cry*in' disgrace
>
> One of *these*
> Surely will *screen* out the sorrow
>
> You should *know*
> How all the *pros* play the game

A similar pattern of assonance links lines in the choruses of "Peg" and "Home at Last":

> Then the shutter *falls*
> You see it *all* in 3D
>
> Well the *dang*er on the rocks is surely past
> Still I re*main* tied to the mast

The matching of vowel sounds also brings coherence to "Josie's" metrically irregular (3, 1, 5, 3, 2, 3, 3) chorus. The long Os in the phrase "Josie comes home" give a ring of inevitability to the opening line, and the word "home" finds a near-mate in the penultimate line's "Roman." The long I string that begins with "pride" continues like so—

> The *live wire*
> She prays *like* a Roman
> With her *eyes* on *fire*

—bolstering memorability through sonority.

Assonance is also at work on the albums surrounding *Aja*. The phrases "*wait*ing for the *taste*" and "*last* pi*aste*r" from *Katy Lied*'s "Doctor Wu" are good examples, as is "*hide* in*side* a hall" from *The Royal Scam*'s "The Caves of Altamira." On *Scam*'s title track, a gloomy tale of Puerto Rican life in urban America, the minute-plus first verse concludes with this assonant passage:

> On the *ri*sing *tide*
> To New York City
> Did they *ride*
> Into the street

Gaucho's "Time Out of Mind" contains three similar spots ("you *bet*ter be *ready*," "*roll*ing in the *snow*," "*light* in my *eyes*"), and *The Nightfly* is a feast of matching vowels:

> There'll be *span*dex *jack*ets

> *Keep* my *squeeze* on *Green* Flower Street

Re*spect* the *sev*en *sec*ond delay we use

To*night* the *night* is *mine*

On the *day* I *came* to *stay*

Other recognizable poetic techniques at work on *Aja* include alliteration ("screen out the sorrow," "dime dancin'," "favorite foreign movie," "serves the smooth retsina," "soulful secret," "hats and hooters," "strike at the stroke"), complex rhyme ("duchess" and "much as," "came ragin'" and "rampagin'"), unconventional rhyme schemes (the ingenious double verse in "Peg" decodes as ABCCDB-AECCDE), simile ("like a gangster," "like a Roman"), anachronism (phoned-in hotel reservations and a "super highway" against the backdrop of ancient Greece; see also Hollywood and Paleolithic Spain in "The Caves of Altamira"), irony (let's face it, those remedies surely *won't* "screen out the sorrow"), anaphora (all of "Aja's" verses begin with "Up on the hill . . . ") and allusion: "Home at Last's" references to "danger on the rocks" and being "tied to the mast" refer to Odysseus's run-in with the Sirens, the singing sea nymphs who lured sailors aground (although "danger on the rocks" sounds like something an international spy would order). "Josie" is a study in using active verbs—break, rev, throw, shine, shake, mix, strike, dance—

to imbue a lyric with energy and urgency. "Aja" and "Home
at Last" stand out because their natural imagery—hill, trees,
sky, sun, sea, shore, rocks, storm—is entirely out of character: the rest of *Aja*, and the Dan canon in general, is steeped
in the language of technology and modern life: consider the
photographic/cinematic (pornographic?) references in
"Peg" or the motorcycle gangspeak in "Josie." Again, these
techniques aren't limited to *Aja*—alliteration, for example, is
alive and well on *Katy Lied* ("from the fourteenth floor,"
"sing that stupid song"), *The Royal Scam* ("rings of rare
design," "bottom of a bad town"), *Gaucho* ("schoolyard
superman," "prickly pear") and *The Nightfly* ("graphite and
glitter," "stars and stripes")—but they achieve their full
flowering there.

One particularly crafty flourish deserves special mention. Enjambment, the spilling of one line's content into the
next line's form, is at least as old as the Romans, but is rare
in popular music. Rarer still is this syntax-straddling variation on the device from the first verse of "Black Cow":

> You were high
> It was a cryin' disgrace
> They saw your face
> On the counter
> By your keys
> Was a book of numbers

It represents a two-way species of enjambment in which a transitional line can belong either to what precedes it or what follows it. "It was a cryin' disgrace! They saw your face on the counter . . . " works, but so does "On the counter by your keys was a book of numbers . . . " That kind of thing doesn't happen by accident, and testifies to Becker and Fagen's thoroughness in wringing every drop of syntactic intrigue from their mini-narratives.

Aja's longest lyric consists of a mere 210 words; it is "Deacon Blues," which by design has gone uncited so far. Arguably Steely Dan's greatest character study, and almost certainly the closest Becker and Fagen (as a team) will ever come to autobiography, it is narrated in a simultaneously hopeful and desperate voice we'll call "first-person angular." The narrator, an aspiring musician who lives vicariously through his freewheeling, doomed jazz idols, longs to leave behind the days when he merely gazed through "the glass" (a window? a whiskey tumbler? Plato's translucent veil?) and to embrace the glamorous world of gambling, drinking, fornicating and, best of all, improvising:

> I'll learn to work the saxophone
> I'll play just what I feel

Notice that his dream is confused from the outset. "Working" the saxophone (with its utilitarian implications) is a long way from playing what you feel. The lyric contains at least a dozen other oppositions: day/night, past/present, reality/dream, victim/hero, contemplation/action, captivity/freedom, knowledge/passion, chance/will, community/individuality, love/lust, domesticity/barbarism, tears/laughter. These underline not only the differences between a real life of quiet desperation and an imagined life of swingin' abandon, but, on a subtler level, the narrator's own internal confusion. He seeks a fresh start, but chooses a path of certain ruin (dying "behind the wheel"). He boasts he's ready for his moment in the spotlight, but has yet to learn the necessary skills. He wants a title of respect—"Deacon" recalls jazz nicknames like "Duke" (Edward Ellington), "Prez" (Lester Young) and "Count" (William Basie)—but idealizes squalor. Though he calls the sax- and sex-crazed denizens of the evening "those of my kind," he's clearly anything but a worldly libertine: his sexual fantasies are "suburban," his dreams of "home sweet home" conventional. "Deacon Blues" is duplicitous, to put it mildly. While extolling the virtues of dying young in a Bird-like blaze of glory, it quietly spells out the idea's fundamental lunacy. (Q: What do Charlie Parker, Bix Beiderbecke, Art Tatum, Lester Young and Jaco Pastorius have in common? A: None of them had a fiftieth birthday.)

A casual listener might be forgiven for pegging "Deacon Blues" as a pop song about the joy of musicmaking—*Cool, the guy just wants to jam!*—especially when something sounding uncannily like sincerity makes a cameo in the fifth verse:

> I cried when I wrote this song
> Sue me if I play too long
> This brother is free
> I'll be what I want to be

But it's the quintessence of Becker and Fagen's wolf-in-sheep's-clothing technique. The more soul-searching the words, the more sprightly the setting.

At least as poetically dense as its neighbors—it's alliterative ("gazed through the glass," "winners in the world"), assonant ("*learn* to *work*," "*laugh*ing *chance*"), figurative ("the expanding man," "like a viper"), hyperbolic ("cover every game in town"), prosodic ("sun goes down" is set on a descending melody) and formally bold (verses one and three are thorny ABCBDEFFE stanzas)—"Deacon Blues" is a classic Becker/Fagen endgame. Like the composers, growing up outside Manhattan but within earshot of bebop's pounding heart, the song's hero senses the possibility of low-rent redemption in the secret world of jazz. Whether he has a prayer of succeeding depends on what he means by "I already bought the dream." He might mean: "I already paid good money for this 1959 Selmer Mark VI tenor." Or: "I have already come to believe—i.e. have already bought into — this dream of freedom." Either way, he's declaring victory a little early; he hasn't yet entered the fray, but he's already hanging the MISSION ACCOMPLISHED banner on the ship's bridge.

If you look for order in a Steely Dan lyric, you will find it. It won't be the pat explanation the "Who's Katy?" types seek, but even when Becker and Fagen are systematically subverting themselves for the devious pleasure of it, they maintain a level of semantic control unique in the world of pop. On *Aja*, by bringing post-Gershwin compositional gusto to post-Dylan subject matter (and filtering it through the lens of post-Nixon America), they made the strange familiar. And vice versa.

GET TO BENDIN' MY EAR
Harmony

In poetics, prosody is the study of the relationship between the meaning of a poem and the sound of a poem, especially where meter is concerned (hands up if you know what iambic pentameter is). In popular music, prosody describes a more general relationship between a song's words and the way they're purposively set to music. That relationship, when worthy of discussion, is usually melodic (in its distinctive opening phrase, for example, Van Heusen and Burke's "But Beautiful" puts the word "funny" on a cheery major ninth a whole tone above the implied destination pitch, and the word "sad" below it on a flattened seventh) or rhythmic (the "lonely winter" in Kern and Hammerstein's "All the Things You Are" feels positively interminable when the phrase-ending word "long" lands on an extended note with two bars to itself). Only rarely does prosody function harmonically: Billy

Strayhorn's "Lush Life," in which the phrase "so sure" is sung over a perfect cadence worlds away from the chromatic push-pull-push-pull surrounding it, is the exception that proves the rule.

One of Steely Dan's lasting innovations was their habitual use of harmonic prosody. From the beginning, they have insisted that pop harmony (a song's vertical axis, its chordal underpinning) should not simply be wallpaper on which melody notes are hung, but a distinct real-time stream with meaning of its own. Listen to the way "Black Cow's" $Ebmaj^7$, a chord related only tangentially to the verse key of C Major and related not at all to the chorus key of A Major, adds to the sense of alienation in the line "Where are you," and the way the subsequent transition chord, an E^{9sus4} that lasts for two measures, gives way to a fresh tonic, $Amaj^9$, emphasizing the narrator's coincident change of mind (if not heart). Listen to the downward pull of the harmony in the chorus of "Deacon Blues": not by accident do its nine consecutive descending chord changes underscore the sax-toting antihero's death wish. Listen to the open fourths and fifths both implicit in the harmony and spelled out in the guitar and horn figures in "Home at Last": they recall pre-Christian music appropriate to the lyric's Homeric conceit. (Becker and Fagen would use the fifths-as-BC trick again on "Babylon Sisters.") On *The Royal Scam*, harmonic prosody had enhanced the line "Could you feel your whole world fall apart and fade away?" (from "Kid Charlemagne") by setting the last five syllables over a syncopated IV-III-II turnaround into the first chorus—you could hear the entropy in the harmony. On *Gaucho*, the line "slide on down" (from "Hey Nineteen") would be set on a $G^{9(\#11)}$ descending darkly back to the chorus's Im chord ($F\#m^7$); the alternative, a C#7, wouldn't have the same downgrade effect. On *The Nightfly*, the line "we're drifting" would be set on a Bm^7, a chord drifting audibly from the recently established key of Bb Major. Even for listeners not doing real-time harmonic analysis as these songs unfold, the meaning of the changes is part of the experience.

Harmonic prosody can also work in reverse. "I guess that I'm the lucky one," intones the road-weary narrator of "Home at Last," but how are we to take his statement at face value when the harmony is advising us otherwise? The phrase takes place over a series of chords that pull the verse's optimistic, churchy cadences back into the darker domain of the relative minor, with the word "lucky" sitting atop a particularly blue, non-diatonic Ab^{13}. "I would always be studying pieces, looking in harmony books," says Fagen. "So sometimes it would be something I'd seen in a book. Or a couple of chords I liked the sound of together. If I was writing something at the time, I'd try it. If Walter and I were working on a lyric, and we needed a certain effect, I'd try something that I thought would enhance the lyric. Or sometimes go counter to the lyric. Just to keep ourselves from getting bored." In the counter-to-the-lyric category, the line

"Can't you see our love will grow" in "I Got the News" not only descends melodically and diminishes dynamically—it also walks down a rickety staircase of quirky quarter-note chord changes that return the song to its C^6 vamp. So much for love's growth. (Yes, it's a bit of a boner joke too.)

Becker and Fagen gave their audience credit for being able to hear, if not harmonically analyze, their twists, turns and subtly shifting colors. Even in an area of harmonic tranquility, like the eight measures of $Bmaj^9$ that make up the intro of "Aja," there are sharp elevenths floating around, hinting at the less stable (and more exotic) Lydian mode. At the top of the double verse in "Deacon Blues," we hear G^6 and F^6, two relatively neutral chords in the key (V^6 and IV^6 in C Major). Halfway through, when the moment comes around again, the two chords recur as a G^{13} and an F^{13} by virtue of the flattened sevenths in the horn voicings. The difference is hard to quantify, but let's say the second pair of changes is 33 percent bluer; it's roughly the difference between having your "back to the wall" and crawling "like a viper." Also, because the sixth chords are part of the composers' pop palette and the thirteenth chords are specific to jazz, the latter pair audibly pulls the narrator a little further down the road from suburbia to the jook joint of destiny.

Steely Dan records contain harmonic motifs, the way other records contain melodic, rhythmic or lyrical motifs. *The Royal Scam* had been conspicuously packed with minor vamps ("The Caves of Altamira," "Green Earrings," "Sign in Stranger," "Haitian Divorce," the title track) and B-sections beginning with IVmaj[7] or functionally similar IIm[7] chords ("Kid Charlemagne," "The Caves of Altamira," "Everything You Did," the title track); *Aja*, by contrast, was Becker and Fagen's half-step record. "I had always thought chords going down in half-steps were corny sounding," says Fagen. "But I think I just decided I was going to do it anyway. The way I was using it I kind of liked, and I realized the reason I liked it was it reminded me of that old swing tune 'Whispering.' And 'Groovin' High' has that downward chromatic progression. So that's similar to the introduction to 'Peg' and 'Deacon Blues.'" Other jazz standards with chromatic architecture include Thelonius Monk's "Well, You Needn't," Duke Ellington's "Caravan" and Dizzy Gilliespie's "A Night in Tunisia." All these would have been familiar to Becker and Fagen. "Deacon Blues" begins with this downgrade sequence—

$$\text{Cmaj}^7 \ \text{G}^2/\text{B} \ | \ \text{Bbmaj}^7 \ \text{F}^2/\text{A}$$

—then repeats it up a whole tone before pausing on the nine-beat deceptive cadence that sets up the verse. "Peg" begins in a similar fashion—

$$\text{G}^{6/9} \ \text{F\#}^{7(\#9)} \ | \ \text{F}^{6/9} \ \text{E}^{7(\#9)} \ | \ \text{Eb}^{6/9} \ \text{D}^{7(\#9)}$$

—but introduces dominant function to every second chord.

"Aja" includes a similar, but strictly parallel, pattern near the end of its repeated solo form—

$$Fm^{11}\ Em^{11}\ |\ Ebm^{11}\ Dm^{11}$$

—and concludes its chorus with another half-step move (Dbmaj$^{7(b5)}$ to Cmaj$^{7(b5)}$). Related but ascending fragments include the setup to Fagen's synthesizer solo in "Home at Last" (Db^9 to D^9), and this juicy intro-ending flourish in "Josie":

$$Ebmaj^7\ E^{7(\#9b13)}\ |\ C/F\ Gb^{maj7(b5)}$$

All these chord sequences flouted prevailing mid-seventies pop trends which dictated progressions should be either diatonic (the Eagles' "One of These Nights," Fleetwood Mac's "Go Your Own Way") or vamps (any number of disco and funk tunes). Steely Dan weren't the only exception—Michael Franks's 1977 bossa-manqué "Down in Brazil" was built on a twenty-four-bar descending cycle with six tonal centers, and Gino Vannelli's 1975 mixed-meter prog-jazz epic "Where Am I Going" had enough chromaticism for a Debussy tone poem—but they were surely the best-known. Even more than their stunning production values, photographically specific lyrics and unconventional instrumentation, their harmonic content was what set them apart. "Most Steely Dan keyboard parts are whole notes and half-notes, occasionally an accent to catch, but basically very simple," points out Steve Khan. The midrange mojo, then, comes from the actual chord changes. The verse melody in "Josie" could have functioned perfectly well over a stock R&B progression made up of Im^7, IV^7 and V^7 chords, but why use three when eight will do? In the Dan canon, and especially on *Aja*, harmony isn't mere framework: it's the thing itself.

BOOK OF NUMBERS
Sidemen

Having long since relinquished any claim to traditional bandhood—touring was out of the question, and all non-writing members except a part-time Denny Dias had left for the Doobie Brothers or oblivion—Steely Dan circa 1977 cast their albums like film directors, using outside talent according to the needs of their narratives. "We were free to hire anyone we wanted from any discipline," says Donald Fagen. "We had used Phil Woods once [on 'Doctor Wu'], and that had worked out really well. We got the bed tracks fairly quickly on *Aja* over at Producer's Workshop, and we figured until someone stopped us, we'd just pay some people." When the sessions were over, *Aja* included the work of several dozen musicians and singers, not counting those whose tracks didn't end up in a final mix. Many of the contributors had appeared on previous Steely Dan records, but some represented a conscious effort by Becker and Fagen to expand their palette for their most expansive and unapologetically jazz-influenced work to date.

Foremost among the Dan neophytes was legendary saxophonist and composer Wayne Shorter, a veteran of Miles Davis's sixties bands and cofounder (with fellow Davis alum Joe Zawinul) of the influential fusion group Weather Report. In contrast to Hollywood-embedded reedmen like Tom Scott and Ernie Watts, Shorter seldom appeared on pop records, and was initially reluctant to work with Steely Dan. "For *Aja*, we asked [producer] Gary Katz to see if Wayne Shorter wanted to play," says Fagen. "The answer came back 'no.' So we mentioned that to Dick LaPalm, the manager of the studio we were working at [Village Recorders]. He knew Wayne from Weather Report, I guess. So he vouched for us. He said, 'These are nice guys, they record here a lot, they seem to like a lot of old jazz records, they talk about Jackie McLean!' So we made up a track and sent Wayne a chart. He said okay, and came in. And he was great. He took some time with it. We did a couple of takes, and he wanted to look at it some more. He said, 'Give me a minute.' He went over to the piano with the chart, and he was over there for a good half an hour messing with scales. Then he came back and did three or four takes, and they were all great." Becker and Fagen must have been pleasantly surprised by Shorter's humility, his willingness to take off the LEGEND hat and work through their changes, like a mere mortal, with the meter running.

Journeyman tenor specialist Pete Christlieb, another consummate improviser whose credentials came principally from the jazz world (notably the bands of Woody Herman and Louis Bellson), became the narrator's alter ego in "Deacon Blues." "We wanted a hard bop player who could just come in and burn through a bunch of unfamiliar changes without having to screw around," says Fagen. "Sometimes at the end of *The Tonight Show* you'd hear this guy and you could tell he could burn through anything. He was a real gunner. So we made a call to *The Tonight Show* and found out it was Pete. We wanted him to play the hero in 'Deacon Blues.'" Christlieb navigated the song's harmonically intricate landscape in a single take, no mean feat considering its multiple tonal centers and chromatic connective tissue. And, true to the songwriters' plan, he brought an authenticity to the track that might have been impossible for a savvier "pop player" used to rounding the edges off of potentially audience-baffling jazz phrases. Most everyone in Katz's Rolodex would have known it was possible to use a Bb pentatonic scale over both an Ebmaj^7 and an E^7 with altered tensions (as sometime Tom Waits sideman Christlieb does in the last two measures of his "Deacon Blues" solo), but it took a bona fide jazzer to actually bust it out when the red light was on.

Joining Shorter on "Aja" was Steve Gadd, arguably the world's most recorded drummer. A superb groove player whose work on records by Paul Simon, David Sanborn and the Brecker Brothers made him a natural choice for a Becker/Fagen session, Gadd was given an assignment no Dan drummer before him had faced: take a solo. In rock, a drum solo is the ultimate indulgence, a live-only spectacle that often facilitates the reattiring of fellow band members—the drummer doesn't need a costume change because he's shirtless—and involves a lot of stick twirling and gratuitous clockwise trips around the toms. By contrast, in small-group jazz, the drummer is part of the ongoing musical conversation, and uses the kit to color as well as to animate. The two extended drum breaks in "Aja," although aggressive, were part of the latter tradition, more Tony Williams than Mick Shrimpton. While catching all the accents in the track's four-bar ostinato, Gadd peppered the rhythmic grid with short, complex bursts of activity, including several signature sixteenth-note-triplet figures incorporating the kick drum and toms. He helped signal to the pop world that Becker and Fagen, the kings of wry understatement, were not averse to a little untethered improvisation. (Compare Gadd's solo on Chick Corea's "Quartet No. 2—Part 2" [1981].)

"He's a very forceful person," says Fagen of Bernard Purdie, the rightfully vainglorious east-coast drummer who chaired "Deacon Blues" and "Home at Last." "When Bernard would move across the room, you had to get out of the way. He was like a bull. If his hip bone managed to glance off yours, you'd go flying. He had a lot of kinetic energy. The problem was, he'd come in, and his first or second take would be perfect. So while everyone else was still figuring out the changes, Bernard would put on his overcoat and say, 'That's it. I'm going home. Just overdub the other guys.' And we'd say, 'Bernard, man, you know, it's not the same. And we're still working on some sections.'" Purdie, who has alleged he played on as many as twenty-one Beatles tracks, never lacked for confidence: he has even been known to do his own small-scale print advertising. "There's the famous story where he would come to a session in the early sixties, and he'd have two signs with him," reported Fagen on Eagle Rock Entertainment's 1999 Classic Albums *Aja* DVD. "And he'd set up these signs. One on one side of the drums would say YOU DONE IT. And the sign on the other side would say YOU HIRED THE HITMAKER, BERNARD 'PRETTY' PURDIE."

Purdie had also played on an early version of "Peg"—in a process drummer Rick Marotta has called "musical bands," Becker and Fagen would often test different rhythm sections on a given song—but Marotta's skipping hi-hat and muscular, less-is-more approach won the day. "That groove came right out of Rick," says Fagen. "He and [bassist] Chuck Rainey just sunk right into it." (Marotta and Rainey had teamed up before, notably on Aretha Franklin's *Let Me in Your Life*.) Guitarist Steve Khan, who was also on the "Peg" tracking date, remembers, "Working with Rick Marotta was always a total thrill for me. He was, in my opinion, New York's greatest drummer for rock and R&B. He was the only guy who rivaled the way certain LA drummers approached those areas of music. Chuck Rainey was great, too. He was totally about serving the song. [On Steely Dan dates] it always seemed like the guitar and keyboard were guinea pigs for the drums and bass. Donald and Walter have thrown out better tracks than most artists ever end up with."

Trumpeter Chuck Findley had worked with virtually every major name in the burgeoning West Coast scene (including Quincy Jones, Earth, Wind & Fire, James Taylor, Boz Scaggs and, as early as 1969, Tom Scott) as well as Bobby "Blue" Bland, one of Fagen's idols, before playing on *Aja*. "Tom Scott wrote all the horns for *Aja*," says Findley, who had undertaken similar duties on *The Royal Scam*. "I played a lot of things in the middle register on that album. On 'Black Cow' I played flugelhorn, which blended perfectly with the tenor and trombone. When we put on the horns, Walter and Donald would have scratch vocals on all the tunes—sometimes completed vocals."

Not for the first time, Michael McDonald was among the vocalists. A Dan regular since 1975, McDonald had provided a foil for Fagen's dour leads starting with the buoyant pre-chorus of *Katy Lied*'s "Bad Sneakers." His airy tenor became the de facto lead in the bridge of "I Got the News" ("Broadway Duchess . . . "), and the dominant color in the backup stack in "Peg." That McDonald, already a star on the basis of the Doobie Brothers' 1976 smash *Takin' It to the*

Streets, was still willing to play second fiddle to Fagen is a testament to both his team-player philosophy and the late-seventies cachet of a Steely Dan album credit. "Amongst players in LA, working on their stuff was a very big deal," confirms guitarist Lee Ritenour. "You'd see guys at other sessions, and they'd be asking, 'Did your solo make it?'" Chuck Rainey says his "presence on the recording of *Aja* has done more for my career than all the other projects put together. *Aja* will go down in history as one of the greatest recordings of organized music, and it would not be so without the genius of Donald Fagen and Walter Becker."

Also in the vocal corps was Tim Schmit, a longtime member of Poco and, by the time of *Aja*'s release, the newest member of the Eagles (Fagen had contributed synth tracks to Poco's 1977 album *Indian Summer* on the eve of Schmit's departure). Although not a household name, Schmit was a good deal more famous than many of his fellow contributors: even with musical resumés a mile long, A-list studio musicians were seldom known outside the wired catacombs of New York and LA. Jim Keltner, one of the most respected drummers in the game, made his Steely Dan debut on "Josie," and, if he lacked for name recognition in middle America, the composers were nonetheless at their reverent best with him. "The garbage can lid [on the instrumental bridge] was Jim Keltner's idea," says Fagen. "We were in awe of him, so anything he wanted to do was good. We didn't even think about it. We just said, 'Quick! Get Jim Keltner a garbage can lid!'"

Keltner had played with John Lennon, Bob Dylan, Harry Nilsson, Randy Newman, Leon Russell and Joe Cocker, among others. His list of credits was exceptional, but not unusual in the Dan camp: *Aja* saxophonist/arranger Tom Scott, who also played the distinctive Lyricon hook on "Peg," was equally road-tested. Scott's previous recordings included Tom Waits's *The Heart of Saturday Night*, Tim Buckley's *Sefronia*, George Harrison's *Extra Texture*, Carole King's *Wrap Around Joy*, Paul McCartney's *Venus and Mars*, Boz Scaggs's *Silk Degrees*, the Grateful Dead's *Terrapin Station* and much of the Joni Mitchell catalog. Multi-instrumentalist Victor Feldman, the only musician other than Becker and Fagen to participate in all seven Steely Dan albums recorded in the seventies, had accumulated at least as many claims to fame, but mostly in the jazz realm: search the discographies of Miles Davis, Cannonball Adderley, Buddy Rich, Stan Getz, Chet Baker, Wes Montgomery, Art Pepper, Herb Ellis and Ella Fitzgerald, and his name will come up.

More startling still were the curricula vitae of players even hardcore Dan fans would have had trouble picking out of a lineup—not solo artists like Joe Sample and Larry Carlton with major-label records, but inarguably integral pieces of the pop, jazz and R&B scenes of the day. Drummer Ed Greene ("I Got the News") had manned the kit for Dizzy Gillespie, Marvin Gaye, B.B. King, Nancy Wilson, Robert Palmer, Phoebe Snow, Stanley Turrentine, the Dramatics, Bobby "Blue" Bland, Diana Ross, Ramsey Lewis, Three Dog Night, Hall & Oates, Seals & Crofts and at least two Franks (Sinatra and Zappa). Keyboardist Paul Griffin, who sang and played Rhodes on "Peg," had recorded with Bob Dylan, Quincy Jones, George Benson, Donny Hathaway, Van Morrison, Aretha Franklin, Paul Simon, King Curtis, Hank Crawford, Grady Tate, Lou Donaldson, Carl Tjader and Elliott "Reeling in the Years" Randall (Griffin had also received a cowriting credit for his work on "The Fez" in 1976). Saxophonist Plas Johnson, known for his lead tenor work on Henry Mancini's *Pink Panther* theme, had played with Oliver Nelson, Nat King Cole, Benny Carter, Blue Mitchell, Tina Turner, Sam Cooke, Bobby Darin, Dr. John, Joe Pass, Gladys Knight, Bobby Hutcherson, Carole King, Ry Cooder, Ray Brown and at least three Franks (Sinatra, Zappa and Capp). Johnson, who had also worked with Steely Dan on *Pretzel Logic* and *The Royal Scam*, had credits dating back to the forties, including a stint with Fagen's future New York Rock and Soul Revue cohort Charles Brown ("Driftin' Blues," "Black Night," "Get Yourself Another Fool"). Drummer Paul Humphrey ("Black Cow"), a member of the American one-hit-wonder club by virtue of his 1971 single "Cool Aid," had many sessions in common with the players above, as well as record dates with the Four Tops, Gene Harris, Kenny Burrell, Carmen McRae, Les McCann, Dusty Springfield, Jimmy Smith, Michael Franks, Al Kooper, Maria Muldaur and T-

Bone Walker. Humphrey, Griffin and company may not have constituted a rock band in any traditional sense, but it's hard to imagine *Aja*'s intricate, effortless-sounding tracks coming from anything but a handpicked phalanx of pros. It was only when Becker and Fagen began using veteran, jazz-proficient studio musicians en masse that they became satisfied with their own recordings.

ANGULAR BANJOES
Guitar

The last vestige of Steely Dan's rock pedigree was a continuing reliance on electric guitar for groove construction and what wasn't yet called "edge." *Aja* featured seven guitarists: Walter Becker, Larry Carlton, Denny Dias, Dean Parks, Steve Khan, Jay Graydon and Lee Ritenour. Carlton and Parks had been in the fold for several years, and doubled as Becker and Fagen's rhythm section liaisons. Dias, a founding member, was now a guest star. Khan, Graydon and Ritenour were fresh meat.

When people trade Steely Dan stories, the subject of the "Peg" solo inevitably comes up. Depending on whom you believe, as many as eight top guitarists tried and failed to execute one chorus of blues acceptable to Becker and Fagen before Graydon, who had played on recent releases by MOR bigwigs Cher (I mean *big* wigs), Barbra Streisand, Paul Anka,

Andy Williams, Olivia Newton-John and the Carpenters, finally stopped the bleeding. "A lot of rumors started because of 'Peg,'" says Fagen. "It was just a blues with that one change-up you had to watch. We were amazed that it was so hard to get someone to do a comfortable-sounding solo over it. Walter tried it first. I liked what he did, as I recall, but he didn't. Maybe there were a couple of awkward spots. I'm sure if he had tried it the next day, it would have been good, but he just didn't like it. So we started calling guys. We figured, well, let's have [Yellowjackets cofounder] Robben Ford come in and do it, and it'll be done. I don't know if he was nervous, but Robben kept playing these furious solos, which is not really like him—he's usually pretty relaxed. I didn't hear any central idea in what he was playing, so we tried to give him a few ideas, and it just wasn't happening. So we're sitting there playing these things back, and we have nothing against using several takes to put something together, but it just wasn't there. After that, it started to get a little silly. We brought in four or five guys. There was a guy whose name I can't remember, who was more of a jazz guitarist. Someone recommended him to us. That guy almost made it, but it reached a certain point and then there was no peak. We were embarrassed for them and for us. We felt silly spending all this money for this one brief blues solo. I can't remember who else tried it. [Some sources suggest Dan vets Elliott Randall and Rick Derringer were among the hopefuls.] Then somebody recommended Jay Graydon. We had-n't heard of him, but he played a lot of sessions. And he came in and essentially knocked it off, as I recall." Graydon recalls a slightly more complex session, consisting of at least an hour of warm-up takes, a break, some harmonic hints from Fagen (regarding which parts of the progression would tolerate blue notes), more passes that led to the distinctive double-stop opening bars, two more thoroughly scrutinized four-bar chunks, and some licks for the fade.

Khan, who was not among the "guitarists who got the livin' crap kicked out of them" attempting the solo, had played rhythm guitar on the beds. "On that session, Donald and Walter hardly said a word to me," says the former Brecker Brothers and Weather Update member. "Almost nothing! I just played what I felt was right for the tune. I thought for certain that they were going to tell me to do something else. After a while, I asked Elliot Scheiner, 'Am I playing anything usable?' He answered, 'Yes, of course, they love what you're doing. Otherwise, you would have heard something.' I think the problem is that, for some artists, when writers start labeling you a genius, it becomes much too heavy a cross to bear. It's some deep psychological shit, but I think it's why they could never finish anything, never let go of anything, never just say, that's enough, let's put it out. Having the unending budgets and the power of guaranteed sales is a license for abuse. How does one follow up on being a genius? Most of us don't have to worry about that."

"One guitar part would take half a day," says Ritenour, who was already an Epic Records solo artist by the time he was able to make it to a Steely Dan date (he was one of two guitarists on "Deacon Blues"). "Walter Becker and Donald Fagen used to come to the Baked Potato to hear me. Donald would sit in the corner and not say much. They had called me for sessions more than a few times, but it was always short notice: 'Can you make it *now*?' I was glad I finally got to work with them, because I was such a fan. They had incredible patience in the studio. They were into the details. They would try slight variations on a part until they liked it, and spend hours manipulating tape, sometimes literally cutting little holes out of the two-inch master. But they were a only a nine out of ten on the perfectionism scale—Barry Gibb and Pink Floyd were even crazier!"

Becker and Fagen weren't obsessing for the sake of it: they knew what they wanted, and were willing to go deep into the night (and ABC's pockets) to get it. "A lot of the [guitarists] we were using weren't used to playing over too many changes," says Fagen. "They were used to playing mostly blues, or playing in chord positions in a folk-like way. We wanted a real melodic, linear, continuous sort of thing like a bebop player would play, and a lot of them just didn't have that skill. So there was a little dissonance there sometimes. We tried to get them to make a transition from chord to chord instead of just switching positions, which because of our background sounded dumb to us. Maybe some of them got a little annoyed because we would paste together what they did, although I don't remember anyone being mad at us at sessions. Sometimes you'd hear something after the fact. There was the Dire Straits guy [Mark Knopfler, who played on *Gaucho*'s "Time Out of Mind"]: he gave an interview and seemed particularly upset. In that case, frankly, we were having a hard time getting anything from him. We loved the way he sounded, and we wanted to have something good on tape when he went home, so we just kept stopping and starting. And finally we did get something we liked. Not much, but enough to use."

MIX Magazine has characterized Steely Dan as "harsh taskmasters," and it's certainly not a voice in the wilderness. But why should that concern Becker and Fagen's audience? No one cares whether the manager is riding his bench players too hard when the team is winning. Long after the pain of the sessions has evaporated, the audio remains, and Steely Dan, like Miles Davis, Duke Ellington and the other great bandleaders to whom they have consistently paid homage, often got more from their soloists than those soloists could summon even for their own projects. Just as Julian "Cannonball" Adderley never scaled the heights of his blowing on Davis's *Kind of Blue* with his own groups, there's nothing in Larry Carlton's catalog that for sheer memorability compares to his solo on Steely Dan's "Kid Charlemagne." There's mad wisdom in yanking creative people out of their comfort zones and asking them to shoot for the moon; the results can be dazzling, even when they're patchwork. No one takes film directors to task for creating fluid scenes from disparate takes. Likewise, making a great record is not always as simple as capturing an extraordinary real-time performance: sometimes it involves masterful integration of the best fragments available. Just ask Jay Graydon, who, despite being one of LA's busiest producer/guitarists, is still being asked about the day he rescued "Peg," four bars at a time.

TALK IT OUT TILL DAYLIGHT
Process

"Hot licks and rhetoric don't count much for nothing," sang Donald Fagen on "Throw Back the Little Ones," the closing track of 1975's *Katy Lied*. If the Steely Dan organization seemed understaffed in the years following the Great Band Member Purge of '75, it remained crowded at the top: supreme executive power was still wielded by Becker, Fagen and Katz ("a most difficult troika if ever there was one," says Steve Khan). The abiding impression among rock journalists was that, like Alfred Hitchcock, whose detailed shooting scripts made actual filming a form of drudgery, Becker and Fagen had everything planned down to the last detail before they began production. This was pure conjecture, of course, as journalists generally weren't allowed at Steely Dan sessions (although *Rolling Stone*'s Robert Palmer got clearance to watch a full day of work on delay settings for a backup vocal in 1980), and no one outside the musical community had ever seen a Dan chart. But data be damned—from polished results, critics inferred persnickety methods.

In fact, Steely Dan records weren't hatched in pre-production. Partially incubated, maybe. "There would be a chart, and we'd usually have a demo," says Fagen. "We weren't using click tracks yet on *Aja*—Bernard Purdie *was* a click. There was more of a blueprint when I did my *Nightfly* record, because that's when I started doing demos using a sequencer, and I could actually hear what the track was going to be like. When we first started, Walter would talk to the rhythm section, and I'd talk to the guys who played chords. It got less rigid as we went along. Also, when we started out we were scared to talk to the older session guys, so a lot of times we'd transmit things through Gary. The first time Chuck and Bernard came in to play, we were terrified of them. Gary knew them from sessions in New York. He could talk sports. The session guys in New York, especially the black guys, used to play this rummy betting game called Tonk. Gary could play Tonk. He knew all that stuff. But it didn't take long for us to start developing some rapport with the musicians. After we had a hit record, and they were on it, they became our pals."

Becker, Fagen and Katz had many lieutenants on *Aja*, among them executive engineer Roger Nichols, frequent tracking and mix engineer Elliot Scheiner, rhythm section co-arrangers Larry Carlton, Dean Parks and Michael

Omartian, and horn arranger Tom Scott. "For the horns, Walter, Tom and myself would have a session at the piano," says Fagen. "I'd sometimes come in with some lines that I liked. A lot of times I'd give Tom the top line and then he'd fill it in. I'd say, 'I really like Oliver Nelson,' and sometimes I'd show him a chord voicing. He'd say, 'I got it.' He knew what we wanted, essentially. He knew the era and he knew the style, and he'd always come in with pretty much what we wanted. If not, we would alter it a little. The thing with Tom was he would wait until the last minute to do it. He was one of those guys who, at least in those days when he was really bopping around town, would just barely get in under the wire, writing the last note as the last microphone was going up. But he always pulled it off."

Becker and Fagen also involved themselves in post-production. They stayed on hand for edits, passed judgment on mastering, collaborated with Katz on sequencing album tracks. On *Aja*, there is a discernible musical logic to the order of the songs: "Black Cow" starts in C Major, the unofficial home key for keyboards, and ends in A Major; beginning an upward trend, "Aja" starts up a whole tone in B Major and ends on a Bm^{11} vamp; "Deacon Blues" starts up a semitone in C Major and ends on a verse-based tag that has a G^6 at the top of the phrase; after the side break (no longer a factor in the digital world), "Peg" starts roughly where Side A finished, with a $G^{6/9}$, and ends with repeated choruses in G Major; "Home at Last" begins the darkening process by changing color but not root, starting and ending in G Minor; "I Got the News" centers around G Minor–related C Mixolydian material; and "Josie" finishes the record in E Minor, the swampiest, least jazzy, most guitar-friendly key possible.

For Becker and Fagen, post-production commitment had its limits. By 1977, the duo had mastered the art of avoiding the commercial requirements of their jobs, touring not at all, doing a minimum of promotion, leaving business decisions to the suits. "Early on we objected to a single they were going to put out from *Katy Lied*, because the first one ['Black Friday'] was a stiff," says Fagen. "We said, 'Let *us* pick the single.' And that one ['Bad Sneakers'] was a stiff as well. After that, we let them do it." Commerce may have been anathema to its creators, but *Aja* did just fine: it shipped gold, sold over three million copies worldwide in its first year, spent fourteen months on the *Billboard* album chart (where it peaked at number 3), went three-for-three in the singles department—"Peg" (number 11 *Billboard*, number 8 *Cash Box*), "Deacon Blues" (number 19 *Billboard*, number 17 *Cash Box*) and "Josie" (number 26 *Billboard*, number 21 *Cash Box*) were the biggest Steely Dan hits since early 1974—and even got props from NARAS, landing in the "Album of the Year" and "Vocal Group" categories at the Grammy Awards alongside commercial juggernauts like *Rumours* and *Hotel California* (awards shows make strange bedfellows). Turns out hot licks and rhetoric *do* count for something.

SOMEBODY ELSE'S
FAVORITE SONG
FM (No Static at All)

Until the seventies, the music business was largely a singles machine. Singles drove album sales, and often existed independently of albums. The really big ones went gold, all by their three-minute selves. Even the Beatles, whose *Sgt. Pepper's Lonely Hearts Club Band* brought new legitimacy to the rock LP and heralded the AOR (album-oriented rock) era, were apt to fill the gaps between major releases with blockbuster 45s: classic sides like "Day Tripper," "We Can Work It Out," "Strawberry Fields Forever," "Penny Lane" and "Hey Jude" were not culled from any of the group's official (UK) albums.

By the time Steely Dan entered the fray, everything had changed. AOR was driving careers. An album could sell into the millions with little help from singles (1971's *Led Zeppelin IV* has gone platinum twenty-three times in the US, and

"Stairway to Heaven," its most recognizable track, has never been released individually). FM rock radio had evolved from a freaky, freeform, low-stakes phenomenon into one of music's chief promotional tools, and, as such, was ripe for ridicule. Steely Dan's opportunity to bite the hand that fed them came when they were invited to write the theme for Universal's *FM*. In the Martin Mull–led comedy, the employees of a Los Angeles rock station stage a coup d'air-waves in an effort to prevent their corporate bosses—the *man*, man—from turning them into shills. The irony was that, by 1978, that battle had already been lost in just about every major market in North America. FM disc jockeys were no longer making programming decisions, burgeoning media syndicates were narrowcasting to their young, white, male demographic, and record companies were dictating policy via disproportionately powerful third-party "inde-pendent promoters." Because rock and roll had been found-ed on rebellion, it served AOR's purposes to maintain an air of underground credibility, but, like today's urban and alter-native outlets, they were inches away from the mainstream.

MCA's two-record *FM* soundtrack disc was crowded with proven platinum rock acts (including the eerily inter-changeable Boston and Foreigner), so it fell to Steely Dan to interject a little wit into the proceedings. Becker and Fagen attacked their assignment with diabolical glee. "FM (No Static at All)" was a tongue-in-cheek, all-night party record in the "Josie" mold. It grooved hard, arguing for shoeless fun and cheap hooch even as it excoriated rock radio for its narrow playlists ("nothing but blues and Elvis") and background utility ("as long as the mood is right"). Its subtitle sounded less like a technical boast than an admission that nothing on the airwaves was likely to surprise anyone. The overlapping voices in the refrain mimicked a generic station ID—Fagen would use the same conceit on *The Nightfly*'s title song—the implication being that, in its haste to wipe out background noise, FM radio had forgotten all about foreground noise.

If "FM" (the lyric) is an argument for adventurousness, "FM" (the record) is an instance of its own doctrine, with twists and turns aplenty. After an overture that goes to some lengths to establish the key of A Major, it settles into a groove—a fourth down, in E Minor. Its swampy, hypnotic vamp, played in Mancini-style parallel fifths by bass and guitar (both Becker), is simple enough, a basic two-bar Dorian figure that sounds like an uptempo Steely Dan groove slowed down to two-thirds speed. In its first statement, it lasts all of seven bars. On the phrase "girls don't seem to care," the harmonic movement begins in earnest, following the melody down stepwise from $Cmaj^7$ to $F\#^7$, then to B^7, and finally to $Emaj^9$. The new tonal center (E Major) is temporary: after one measure, and a transitional A^{13} chord, we find ourselves in B Major. This key, too, lasts but one measure: an Am^9-to-Em^9 cadence reestablishes E Minor, then an A/C# once again hints at E Dorian. A standard minor-blues turnaround brings us back to the top of the phrase, and we find ourselves, eight lines into the song, having heard four key changes, some cuíca and marimba by Victor Feldman, and a string section arranged and conducted by none other than Hollywood veteran Johnny Mandel. (If that sounds like a recipe for late-seventies corporate rock, your Styx albums were different from mine.)

The journey above represents only half of "FM's" double verse. The second time we get to the $Emaj^9$, the activity remains diatonic to E Major for several bars, clearing the way for the hook—

> No static at all
> No static at all
> FM
> No static at all

—which is something more than a tag line and less than a chorus. The "first ending" never recurs. Tenorman Pete Christlieb, fresh from his "Deacon Blues" triumph, solos over a new harmonic chunk related to the song proper, but containing fresh material. An Em^9 and A^{13} suggest E Dorian is still in effect, but, in addition to functioning as I and IV in that mode, they become, by implication, II and V when the progression shifts into D Major for a four-bar chromatic descent related to the intros of "Peg" and "Deacon Blues." Christlieb gets additional room to improvise on "FM (Reprise)," a three-minute instrumental comprising the solo from the single plus another fifty or so bars of inventive blowing. In one noteworthy spot, he ends up stating a fully formed F blues lick over the E Minor vamp, selling it through sheer melodic logic and rhythmic momentum. "FM (Reprise)" was the B-side of the single, and was included (along with the Dan's first hit, 1972's "Do It Again") on the *FM* soundtrack. After a restatement of the second verse and refrain, the A-side's tag is decorated with Becker's bluesy guitar fills, the track's most AOR-sounding element.

"FM (No Static at All)" became *Aja*'s de facto third single, wedged as it was between "Deacon Blues" and "Josie" on the release schedule. Many a casual fan assumed the track was from the current Steely Dan album. AM stations, unaware of the lyric's ironic undercurrent, cut the "A" from "Aja" into the "F" hole so they could play the track without promoting the stereo competition. The ultimate irony was that FM radio, champion of the long-playing record, had as its anthem a one-off single.

YOU KNOW HOW TO HUSTLE
Fallout

The music business went into blockbuster mode in the late seventies, when a slew of multiplatinum records—*Frampton Comes Alive!, Saturday Night Fever, Boston, Bat Out of Hell, Hotel California, Grease, Rumours*—proved there was more money to be made hawking mainstream pop than anyone had previously imagined (the movie business equivalents were *Jaws* and *Star Wars*). Signs of hubris were everywhere: Elton John released his second *Greatest Hits* less than two years after his first *Greatest Hits*; the Village People were immortalized on a double live album; all four members of Kiss put out solo records on the same day; Barbra Streisand did Judy Garland; Donna Summer did Richard Harris; the Bee Gees did the Beatles. Within a few years the business would be reeling from a double-digit dip in sales (owing to both the sagging economy and the disco implosion), but while Gibbmania was still in effect, *Aja* incongruously appeared. And killed.

ABC had a Steely Dan *Greatest Hits* package on the street in time for the 1978 Christmas rush, within a week of "Josie's" last appearance on the *Billboard* Hot 100. The double disc went platinum within days. As a crash course in the Dan, it was flawed—"Deacon Blues" was missing, and *Pretzel Logic* was overrepresented—but it let the hits-only crowd in on core Becker/Fagen material like "Bodhisattva," "Bad Sneakers," "Doctor Wu" and "Kid Charlemagne." More intriguing to serious fans was the inclusion of that rarest of rarities, a fully realized, previously unreleased Steely Dan track. "Here at the Western World," originally recorded for *The Royal Scam* in 1976, detailed life behind the scenes at a brothel: if you knew the secret knock, Ruthie (the madam) would provide a key to a room in which a skinny girl would provide "the sweetness you've been cryin' for," all for the thrifty-even-by-seventies-standards price of a Jackson (twenty bucks). Denizens of the Western World included "the mayor and all his friends," an unconscious sailor and someone called Klaus (conceivably a reference to Nazi war criminal Klaus Barbie, then in hiding in South America). Background vocals were added to the track in preparation for its release, but the 1976 arrangement featuring Bernard Purdie, Chuck Rainey, Michael Omartian, Dean Parks and Jeff Mironov was otherwise intact. (Point of interest: cyberpunk author and avowed Dan fan William Gibson references "Here at the Western World" in his 1996 novel *Idoru*.)

Among the side projects Becker and Fagen undertook in *Aja*'s wake, Woody Herman's *Chick, Donald, Walter & Woodrow* (1978) may well have been closest to their hearts. Side A of the record was a three-part suite written by Chick Corea. Side B consisted of contemporary big band arrangements of five late-model Steely Dan tunes ("Aja," "Green Earrings," "Kid Charlemagne," "FM" [listed without its parenthetical title] and "I Got the News" [incorrectly listed as "*I've* Got the News"]). The composers handpicked the material with Herman, then sixty-five, a feisty composer and woodwind player who had led two of the top bands of the forties and given early exposure to tenor giants Stan Getz, Zoot Sims and Gene Ammons. The results were mixed—a big band playing funk can sound dangerously close to cop show music—but Becker and Fagen had crossed creative paths with another jazz hall-of-famer, and that was an end in itself. The presence of Dan regulars Tom Scott and Victor Feldman, as well as future *Down Beat* poll topper Joe Lovano, enlivened the proceedings.

Becker and Fagen had more hands-on involvement with Pete Christlieb and Warne Marsh's *Apogee*: they produced the dueling tenors record for Warner Brothers, and contributed an original, "Rapunzel," to its repertoire. Christlieb and Marsh, a generation apart and both heirs to the west coast school, did not treat the date as a pissing contest: though the improvising was intense and harmonically rigorous throughout, at no point did the coleaders get in each other's way or lapse into one-upmanship. And with Nichols and Scheiner engineering, Becker and Fagen were in their comfort zone. "Rapunzel" belonged to the bebop tradition of composing new melodies—"heads," in the parlance—over the changes of existing tunes. Charlie Parker's "Ornithology" is based on "How High the Moon"; Tadd Dameron's "Hot House" is based on "What Is This Thing Called Love?"; Sonny Rollins's "Oleo" is based on "I Got Rhythm." The harmonic structure of "Rapunzel" comes from a 1964 Bacharach/David tune called "In the Land of Make Believe" (recorded by the Drifters with Leiber and Stoller producing, perfected by Dusty Springfield on her landmark *Dusty in Memphis* album). It begins on an Ab^7 chord, hints at the distinctive raised-fourth-to-major-third melodic fragment that characterized the original, then resolves to a C^6, the tonic. This rather exotic move—the Ab^7 requires a "Lydian Flat 7" scale that contains only three pitches diatonic to C—happens twice before the second eight begins. The latter section starts conventionally on an Am^7 (the relative minor of C), but, true to *Aja*'s modus operandi, within three bars we find ourselves on the new, if fleeting, tonal center of D major (the modulation, similar to the one in "Deacon Blues" that links the choruses to the re-intros, must have been part of the composers' attraction to the Bacharach progression). After a II-V back into C, the changes seem to set up a resolution to Am, making the Ab^7 at the top of the second statement sound all the more peculiar.

Becker and Fagen were beginning to realize their sensibilities were portable. When Gary Katz got singer-songwriter Marc Jordan signed to Warner Brothers in 1978, Fagen decided to take an active role in making Jordan's debut for the label, *Mannequin*. "Gary was my producer, and on certain songs he would bring Donald in," says Jordan. "Walter dropped in once or twice, but Donald would come down and actually work on stuff: play Rhodes, do synth solos, arrange on the fly. He absolutely reharmonized some of the songs, like 'Jungle Choir.' That one became clustery and dark just by virtue of Donald's voicings. He had real musical weight to him. What he played always had this luscious darkness." Jordan's previous recordings had been for CBS Records in Toronto. Accustomed to playing his material onstage, and definitely unaccustomed to six-figure album budgets, Jordan took some time to adapt to the Steely Dan team's high-tech, piecemeal approach. "I was really a live singer," says Jordan. "And Roger Nichols was such a technical genius. He had this incredible dexterity on the board. He was like a machine. He could put his ten fingers on ten faders, and just start mixing, with every finger moving independently. And he could punch *anything*. Gary was more laid back, more of a facilitator."

"We started out using Elton John's band—James Newton Howard, Davey Johnstone, those guys—but it didn't really work out. That's when Jeff Porcaro was brought in, and Chuck Rainey, Victor Feldman, Larry Carlton." In addition to the nucleus of what had only recently become Toto (besides Porcaro, keyboardist David Paich and guitarist Steve Lukather were aboard), *Mannequin*'s liner notes wound up including Dean Parks, Clydie King, Paul Griffin, Tim Schmit and Tom Scott. "Roger ended up mixing the record," says Jordan. "He was not originally supposed to; Elliot [Scheiner] was much more of a finesse mixer. But at a certain point we ran out of money. I always felt the mixes were too thin and dry. They never sounded good on the radio to me." Jordan remained in the LA fold, however, and wound up working with Jay Graydon—and Michael Omartian, Jim Keltner, Pete Christlieb and Chuck Findley— on his second Warner album, *Blue Desert*. Fagen would be listed as a player on early-eighties recordings by Rickie Lee Jones, David Sanborn and Diana Ross.

In the music business, success is the equivalent of blood in the water. ABC showed admirable restraint in keeping their list of *Aja* cash-ins to two: in addition to the *Greatest Hits* package, the label released a "+ Four" twelve-inch EP containing "Do It Again," "Haitian Divorce" and two long-out-of-print, pre–*Can't Buy a Thrill* songs from 1972 called "Dallas" and "Sail the Waterway" (both expendable proto-Dan relics, but of interest to devotees). Not so the indy labels. Just as "Peg" was peaking, a small company called Visa Records reissued the Becker/Fagen soundtrack to an obscure 1971 hippy comedy called *You've Got to Walk It Like You Talk It or You'll Lose That Beat*. The film featured comedian Richard Pryor (as a wino) and future *Barney Miller* series regular Steve Landesberg (as a men's room attendant), but was of historical interest only because of its original music. Written by Becker and Fagen under the auspices of their short-lived production deal with Jay and the Americans' Kenny Vance, the seven songs had era-appropriate titles like "Roll Back the Meaning" and "If It Rains," and included guitar work by future Steely Dan cohort Denny Dias. The long-forgotten soundtrack's 1978 reappearance was greeted by the composers with mortification, the kind thirty-year-olds experience when their mothers haul out their high school yearbooks. Later compilations featuring Becker and Fagen's early demos (*Sun Mountain, Berrytown, Old Regime, Stone Piano, Roaring of the Lamb, Catalyst, Pearls of the Past, The Early Years*) triggered similar embarrassment.

In the post-*Aja* oddities category, fans are advised to check out the Jacksons' "Jump for Joy." The track, from the Gamble and Huff–produced *Goin' Places* (released in October 1977, about a month after *Aja*), was cowritten by longtime Philadelphia International keyboardist Dexter Wansel, and has striking similarities to "Peg." To begin with, it is organized around a keyboard/guitar figure whose dotted-eighth rhythm is identical to the one in "Peg," and whose harmonic content is virtually the same: the opening phrase of the chorus in "Jump for Joy" decodes as IV, I/III, II, I, while the same spot in "Peg" decodes as IV, I/III, II, VI, the last chord being functionally similar to a tonic. Also, the key (G Major) is the same, and the tempo is mighty close. The resemblance is surely in the realm of coincidence, though: although *Goin' Places* came out after *Aja*, turning a knockoff around in a month would have required spies at Steely Dan sessions earlier in the year, and a record pressing plant capable of defying the laws of physics. It should also be noted that producers Kenny Gamble and Leon Huff, having pretty much owned America's airwaves since 1972, were anything but hard-up for ideas.

Becker and Fagen concluded the *Aja* chapter of their career by moving back to New York. There they began crafting *Gaucho*, an album that would prove even more costly and challenging to complete. The pressure, insofar as it mattered to Steely Dan, was on: in the era of the blockbuster, each release had to be bigger than the last.

THOSE OF MY KIND
Historical Moment

"A band like Steely Dan couldn't get arrested now," former Dan guitarist and current US Department of Defense consultant Jeff Baxter opined back in 1995. Indeed, the conditions necessary for the success of a band with Steely Dan's history, personnel and goals seem to be specific to the seventies. Three main factors were in play: the confluence of jazz and rock; unprecedented stylistic breadth in pop radio; and a record business temporarily open to new forms of expression.

Jazz and rock were considered strange bedfellows when they began cross-pollinating in the late sixties. Purists on both sides of the argument had lost track of the fact that both forms of music were blues-based American art forms with a common heritage of improvisation and rebellion. Chuck Berry could swing; Lionel Hampton could rock.

Miles Davis, always among the catalysts in jazz's transformations, had begun using electric instrumentation on *In a Silent Way*, the 1969 album often cited as jazz fusion's fountainhead. In the years that followed, several of Davis's sidemen became prime movers in the fusion movement: Chick Corea with Return to Forever, Joe Zawinul and Wayne Shorter with Weather Report, Herbie Hancock with the Head Hunters, Tony Williams with Lifetime, and John McLaughlin with the Mahavishnu Orchestra. Fusion merged funk grooves, rock aggression and jazz harmony. Its extended compositions were known to take up entire album sides (Miles started that, too), and Cuban, Brazilian, Indian and other world music crept in occasionally. When Weather Report's eponymous debut became one of the most anticipated releases of 1971 in any genre, the jazz establishment began to take notice. Meanwhile, groups from the commercial side of the tracks had taken up the cause. Chicago, Blood, Sweat and Tears, Chase and Lighthouse boasted permanent horn sections, and were categorized frequently as (horrors!) jazz rock. Earth, Wind and Fire, the brainchild of former Ramsey Lewis drummer Maurice White, applied the model to funk. Bay Area Bill Graham protégées Tower of Power did likewise.

Into this evolving stew came Steely Dan. Walter Becker and Donald Fagen had ventured west in 1971, at the urging of producer Gary Katz. Katz had been hired as a staffer by ABC/Dunhill Records in Los Angeles, and insisted the label also hire Becker and Fagen as songwriters. The transplanted New Yorkers gave work-for-hire songwriting the old college try, even placing "I Mean to Shine" on Barbra Streisand's Richard Perry–produced 1971 album *Barbra Joan Streisand*, but they soon tired of trying to shoehorn their vision into easily coverable units (ABC/Dunhill's roster included Three Dog Night, Steppenwolf, the Grass Roots, the Mamas & the Papas and the James Gang). They convened the original Steely Dan lineup during their off hours.

Can't Buy a Thrill was not a fusion record, not by a long shot. But it got the attention of jazz and crossover audiences by virtue of its harmonically rich songwriting, crisp playing and obvious jazz awareness. "Do It Again," the first single, had a Santana-style groove and two lengthy solos. "Reeling in the Years," the follow-up, was a skittering, meticulous shuffle with two blistering Elliott Randall breaks that immediately caught the ear of not only jazz-schooled listeners, but one Jimmy Page. Owners of the LP found additional intriguing content within, including the serpentine "Fire in the Hole." Still, it wasn't fusion. For one thing, it was vocal, and song-based, and fusion was almost never those things: Return to Forever vocalists Flora Purim and Gayle Moran aside, fusion was a player's genre. For another, *Can't Buy a Thrill* wasn't that tricky rhythmically: with the exception of the occasional dropped beat or two (there's a bar of three before the chorus of "Dirty Work," for example), it was a 4/4, toe-tappin' affair. Then there were its comparatively conventional aims. While leaving plenty of space for instrumental breaks, Steely Dan never crossed the line—let's call it the ELP threshold—between invention and pretension.

As Becker and Fagen went forward from 1972, the sound of their records did approach fusion on occasion—the opening section of 1975's "Your Gold Teeth II" comes to mind—but they remained, by design, in a grey area they alone had staked out. When they rocked, it was usually with duplicitous intent: "Parker's Band," one of their most uptempo guitar-based workouts, was a panegyric for a jazz musician ("Bring your horn along," it beckoned). Conversely, when they swung, they were often at their toughest: "Bodhisattva" and "Pretzel Logic" weren't for sissies. When they settled into a funk vamp, they weren't selling groove alone: "Green Earrings" is a jagged, minimalist tract whose basic riff ends up supporting all manner of chromatic displacement and rhythmic trickery. And *Aja*, their most jazz-infused album, was also their hookiest and most commercially successful.

In short, Steely Dan were courting neither Chick and Herbie's audience nor Peaches and Herb's. It felt wrong to call them jazz rock, but calling them pop seemed somehow insufficient. Still, it's hard to imagine a better era for them than the seventies. Fusion wasn't a perfect synthesis of its constituent elements—wasn't, in the end, a fusion at all—but it kept the chatter about jazz v. rock alive long enough for Becker and Fagen to sneak through a temporary window of opportunity, and gave those so inclined a label for too-elaborate-to-be-pop records like *Aja* and *Gaucho*.

By 1977, AM radio was nearing the end of its reign as the vehicle by which the Top 40 took shape and was disseminated. FM, with its static-free stereo signal, would soon enough supplant traditional hit-radio stations in the major cities of America (it would take longer in Canada because federal regulations prohibited narrow FM playlists). And once that had happened, formatting, the destructive parsing of radio markets into demographically discrete chunks, would begin in earnest. By the end of the eighties, AC, CHR, AOR, MOR, classic rock, modern rock and other narrowcast formats had sought, and mostly found, their market shares. No longer was radio "charged with the resonating echoes of tribal horns and antique drums," as McLuhan had put it back in 1964: now the sounds on any given station were not for all the villagers—just the villagers whose income and spending habits matched the sales department's bloodless mission statements.

The casualty was diversity. During AM's salad days, playlists were assembled with little regard for what music belonged together stylistically or, especially, demographically. A Top 40 station in the seventies could play mainstream pop (Player's "Baby Come Back"), disco (Chic's "Dance, Dance, Dance"), punk (the Ramones' "Rockaway Beach"), singer-songwriter fare (Jackson Browne's "Running on Empty"), bubblegum (Leif Garrett's "Put Your Head on My

Shoulder"), funk (Parliament's "Flash Light"), novelties (Randy Newman's "Short People"), blue-eyed soul (Boz Scaggs's "Hollywood"), Britpop (ELO's "Sweet Talkin' Woman"), orchestral music (John Williams's "Theme from *Close Encounters of the Third Kind*"), R&B (Raydio's "Jack and Jill"), MOR (B.J. Thomas's "Everyone Loves a Rain Song"), country (Waylon and Willie's "Mammas Don't Let Your Babies Grow Up to Be Cowboys"), folk (Gordon Lightfoot's "The Circle Is Small"), smooth jazz (Chuck Mangione's "Feels So Good"), hard rock (Kiss's "Rocket Ride"), soft rock (Andrew Gold's "Thank You for Being a Friend"), corporate rock (Foreigner's "Long, Long Way from Home"), glam rock (the Sweet's "Love Is Like Oxygen"), roots rock (Eric Clapton's "Lay Down Sally"), southern rock (Lynyrd Skynyrd's "What's Your Name") and progressive rock (Kansas's "Dust in the Wind"). In fact, all the songs above were on the *Billboard* singles chart on March 4, 1978, the week "Peg" peaked. Sure, it was impossible for anyone to like *all* of it, but at least it wasn't defined by what it excluded—at least popular music was still a shared cultural experience with porous boundaries.

The upside to a pan-categorical pop chart for an artist like Steely Dan was that classification wasn't the first order of business. As long as a track was "getting good phone" (garnering frequent requests), it didn't much matter whether it was similar to the tracks before and after it. The June 10, 1978, Hot 100 found "Deacon Blues" wedged between

"Because the Night" (Patti Smith's collaboration with Bruce Springsteen) and "Use Ta Be My Girl" (the last Top 10 hit of the O'Jays' extraordinary Philadelphia International streak). A little over two months later, "Josie" was flanked by "Beast of Burden" (the second single from the Rolling Stones' *Some Girls*) and "Almost Like Being in Love" (Michael Jackson's cover of the 1947 Lerner and Loewe chestnut). The permutations were infinite: while waiting for Andy Gibb to come on, an impressionable listener might have been exposed to a little Steely Dan. In the current era of unchecked media consolidation and consulted-to-death radio, divisions form early: you wind up with Gwen Stefani fans who have never heard Radiohead, when a truly robust Top 40 could tolerate both. There are late-model boomers— *they walk among us*—who remember when you didn't have to change the station to hear James Brown, Van Morrison, Led Zeppelin, Gladys Knight, Neil Young, Steely Dan—pop's full length and breadth—in an afternoon. "Don't touch that dial," went the battle cry of frenetic disc jockeys everywhere, and it was, at one time, decent advice.

Pop radio's eclecticism forced record companies' A&R departments to keep their ears open. If Glen Campbell, the Staple Singers and the Average White Band could have number-one pop records in the same year, nothing was far-fetched. In Steely Dan's case, the big signing came from an "inside man" (Katz), but Becker and Fagen's continued success owed something to the seventies' climate of tolerance.

Yes, there was number-crunching going on, but in trying to justify funding an almost-fusion group, a late-seventies music executive could point to actual chart successes like Miles Davis's *Bitches Brew* (number 35), Herbie Hancock's *Head Hunters* (number 13), the Crusaders' *Southern Comfort* (number 31), Weather Report's *Heavy Weather* (number 30), Return to Forever's *Romantic Warrior* (number 35), Jean-Luc Ponty's *Enigmatic Ocean* (number 35), Billy Cobham's *Crosswinds* (number 23), Stanley Clarke's *School Days* (number 34) and George Duke's *Reach for It* (number 25). The record business's permissiveness was born of necessity: people were actually supporting new styles and substyles.

So Jeff Baxter, likely the only Pentagon regular nick-named "Skunk," had it right in 1995. The conditions that allowed Steely Dan's unique amalgam of jazz, rock and R&B to flourish in the seventies have not recurred, and likely won't. Jazz and its offshoots have achieved permanent niche status. Pop radio has splintered into a half-dozen specialized formats. And the music business, hemorrhaging cash as it struggles to persevere in a broadband world, has returned to priority one: finding round pegs for round holes.

LAY DOWN THE LAW
AND BREAK IT
Conclusion

"Most people in pop music never think about development, unless it's louder and faster," says Donald Fagen. (In most cases, the "louder" is intentional, and the "faster" isn't.) Steely Dan emerged during the twilight of the golden age of AM radio, when listeners expected tight little eight-bar verses (A) to lead into tight little eight-bar choruses (B), with the occasional bridge (C) for variation—think "Ticket to Ride" or "(Sittin' on) The Dock of the Bay." And, apart from exceptions like "Bodhisattva" (AA), "Black Friday" (AAA) and "Your Gold Teeth" (AABA), Becker and Fagen had mostly toed the line when it came to modern pop structure. But *Aja* saw them pushing the envelope like never before. While the verse-chorus paradigm was still in effect, especially on the hits, there were variations aplenty. The seven tracks break down formally like this (if you're counting bars, bear in mind that "Home at Last" is in cut time):

Black Cow
INTRO [8 bars]
VERSE 1a [7 bars]
VERSE 1b [9 bars]
CHORUS [12 bars]
VERSE 2a [7 bars]
VERSE 2b [9 bars]
CHORUS—variation [12 bars]
ELECTRIC PIANO SOLO [18 bars]
CHORUS—abbreviated [8 bars]
TAG W/ TENOR SOLO [approx. 30 bars]

Aja
INTRO [8 bars]
VERSE 1a [10 bars]
VERSE 1b [8 bars]
REFRAIN—includes 3/4 bar [8 bars]
RE-INTRO [4 bars]
VERSE 2a [10 bars]
VERSE 2b [8 bars]
REFRAIN [8 bars]
BREAK [2 bars]
VAMP [8 bars]
INSTR. BRIDGE 1a—includes 2/4 bar [8 bars]
INSTR. BRIDGE 1b—variation [10 bars]
INTERLUDE 1—includes 3/4 and 2/4 bars [12 bars]

VAMP [4 bars]
INSTR. BRIDGE 2a—includes 2/4 bar [8 bars]
INSTR. BRIDGE 2b—variation [10 bars]
INTERLUDE 2—variation [16 bars]
TENOR/DRUM SOLO I—includes 2/4 bar [17 bars]
TENOR/DRUM SOLO II—includes 3/4 bar [17 bars]
RE-INTRO [8 bars]
VERSE 3a [10 bars]
VERSE 3b [8 bars]
REFRAIN [8 bars]
TAG W/ DRUM SOLO [approx. 32 bars]

Deacon Blues
INTRO—includes 5/4 bar [6 bars]
VERSE 1a [16 bars]
VERSE 1b [16 bars]
CHORUS [18 bars]
RE-INTRO [4 bars]
VERSE 2a [16 bars]
VERSE 2b [16 bars]
CHORUS [18 bars]
RE-INTRO—harmonic variation [4 bars]
TENOR SOLO [20 bars]
RE-INTRO [6 bars]
VERSE 3—"B" changes [16 bars]
CHORUS [18 bars]

RE-INTRO [4 bars]
TAG W/ TENOR FILLS [approx. 40 bars]

Peg
INTRO [8 bars]
VERSE 1 [12 bars]
VERSE 2 [12 bars]
CHORUS [10 bars]
INTERLUDE [2 bars]
RE-INTRO [8 bars]
GUITAR SOLO [12 bars]
VERSE 3 [12 bars]
CHORUS [8 bars]
CHORUS [8 bars]
CHORUS W/ GUITAR FILLS [8 bars]
CHORUS W/ GUITAR FILLS [8 bars]
TAG W/ GUITAR SOLO [approx. 6 bars]

Home at Last
INTRO [16 bars]
VERSE 1 [16 bars]
CHORUS [16 bars]
RE-INTRO [8 bars]
VERSE 2 [16 bars]
CHORUS [16 bars]
RE-INTRO [8 bars]

INTERLUDE [8 bars]

SYNTH SOLO [8 bars]

GUITAR SOLO [16 bars]

CHORUS [16 bars]

TAG W/ GUITAR SOLO [approx. 32 bars]

I Got the News

INTRO [8 bars]

VERSE 1a [8 bars]

REFRAIN [4 bars]

VERSE 1b [4 bars]

INTRO VAMP [2 bars]

BREAK [2 bars]

INTRO VAMP [4 bars]

VERSE 2a [8 bars]

REFRAIN [4 bars]

VERSE 2b [4 bars]

INTRO VAMP—with horns [16 bars]

NEW VAMP [4 bars]

BRIDGE 1 [12 bars]

GUITAR SOLO—bridge 1 changes [12 bars]

INTRO VAMP [4 bars]

BRIDGE 2a [4 bars]

INTRO VAMP [4 bars]

BRIDGE 2b [4 bars]

INTRO VAMP [4 bars]

GUITAR SOLO—Bridge 2 changes [4 bars]
INTRO VAMP [4 bars]
REFRAIN [4 bars]
VERSE 3b [4 bars]
INTRO VAMP [4 bars]
TAG [approx. 29 bars]

Josie
INTRO [8 bars]
VAMP [8 bars]
VERSE 1 [16 bars]
CHORUS [8 bars]
VAMP [4 bars]
VERSE 2 [16 bars]
CHORUS [8 bars]
INTERLUDE [8 bars]
GUITAR SOLO [16 bars]
CHORUS [8 bars]
RE-INTRO—3 extra beats [8 bars]
TAG W/ GUITAR FILLS [approx. 27 bars]

Suffice it to say that's not the roadmap Bob Seger and the Silver Bullet Band were using at the time. All seven songs, while showing signs of rock-and-roll organization, have sections that belong to the big-band era and even older models: the epic "Aja" conforms more to sonata form than Sinatra form. In "Black Cow," "Aja" and "Deacon Blues," the chord changes in the instrumental sections represent new material: Becker and Fagen were not content to have their soloists simply noodling on verse changes or one-chord vamps. This made for very few repeat signs—the rhythm charts for "Aja" required three music stands per player—but, per Fagen's comment above, a sense of thematic development was unmistakable, even in instrumental sections many bands would treat as glorified pee breaks. In fifties and sixties small-group jazz, the so-called "blowing changes" represented a simplified version of the harmony (Oliver Nelson's "Stolen Moments," for example, becomes a straight-ahead minor blues during the solos). In a Steely Dan song, the reverse was often true.

Still, the feel of small-group jazz is all over *Aja*, right from the opening bars of "Black Cow": no one in the ensemble sounds like he's in a hurry to fill space, Larry Carlton's clean, thirdless thirteenth chords placidly ring off in the left speaker, and you find yourself hoping ex-Zappa drummer Paul Humphrey has a good back rest on his throne—that's how far back he's sitting on the beat. On *Aja* (and later *Gaucho*), Steely Dan indulged their penchant for laid-back grooves like never before. They were sometimes hard pressed to get the essence of their dilatory rhythmic tastes across, even to their crack bands. "There were songs where I would anticipate having problems because what I wanted [rhythmically] was so specific," says Fagen. "What I wanted was essentially an anachronism. The musicians were no longer playing that way." Listen to the horn section state the head of Nelson's "Yearnin'" on *The Blues and the Abstract Truth* (1961) for an indication of just how far back four people can lean simultaneously without falling down. Then, if you're not woozy, you may be ready to hear Dexter Gordon play "Ruby, My Dear."

Becker and Fagen's compulsion to run their steely rock and roll machine on jazz fuel may seem counterintuitive, and it's true their retro bent has alienated as many people as it's drawn in over the years, but for those whose pleasure centers are tickled by the likes of *Aja*, the composers' jazz influence is central to the enjoyment. And to the intrigue. Sure, at every Dan show there's a guy screaming for album cuts from *Can't Buy a Thrill*, wishing like hell he could make the brass-reinforced, coed, multiracial twelve-piece ensemble in front of him fit his picture of "classic rock." But he's atypical. To their core fans, Steely Dan are something on the order of a paradigm shift that, for some reason, happened to only one band. There's a big charge to be had in hearing multiple streams of twentieth-century popular art—swing, bebop, postbop, blues, art song, modal jazz, funk, soul, fusion, psychedelic rock, musical theater, science fiction, beat poetry—intertwining without regard for anything but ending up with a complex, *beautiful* result. The latter quality is key. Among the seventies popular music figures who can be said to have made a lasting international impact in their chosen genres (Bob Marley, Bruce Springsteen, David Bowie, Neil Young, Led Zeppelin, Joni Mitchell, Kraftwerk, Brian Eno, David Byrne, maybe Patti Smith and the Clash), only Steely Dan strove consistently to craft things of polished, incontrovertible beauty. If those things frequently turned in on themselves, creating Möbius strip–like impossibilities, their surfaces were nonetheless slick, detailed, machine-tooled and made to thrill—unapologetically so. Songs like "Black Cow" have it both ways: they paint their arid cityscapes in such bold, confident strokes, it's difficult to feel the grimness within. Like a Steve Reich piece or a Miles Davis quintet recording, they make you feel at home in the big, self-conscious, modern world.

Rock critics, generally nonmusicians and therefore the first to look for answers on a lyric sheet, have frequently been stymied by Becker and Fagen's nonconfessional, noncombative tracts. They have accused the duo of being pedants, obfuscators and other unsavory-sounding things. For ambiguity-tolerant Dan fans, though, attempting to translate Beckerandfagenese back into English is something of a sport. A glossary-style site called the Steely Dan Dictionary lets users in on the slang and forgotten brand names with which Becker and Fagen strew their songs; it'll tell you what a "Lark" is (see "I Got the News") in the event you're unfamiliar with the Studebaker Packard Corporation's 1959 line of fine automobiles. The Steely Dan lyric interpretation website Fever Dreams has seen answers like "a

Vietnam veteran," "a mental institution," "Capitol Hill," "an EST retreat," "usurious music execs," "Minton's Playhouse" and "a brothel" in response to this burning question:

What is the song "Aja" about?

The only possible answer is, and will always be, "About eight minutes."

Album Credits

Produced by Gary Katz

Words and Music by Walter Becker and Donald Fagen
All selections 1977 ABC/Dunhill Music, Inc. (BMI)

Lead Vocals: Donald Fagen

Horns arranged and conducted by Tom Scott
Saxes/Flutes: Jim Horn, Bill Perkins, Wayne Shorter, Pete Christlieb,
    Plas Johnson, Tom Scott, Jackie Kelso
Brass: Chuck Findley, Lou McCreary, Slyde Hyde

Rhythm charts prepared by Larry Carlton, Dean Parks and Michael
    Omartian in collaboration with the composers

Engineers: Roger Nichols, Elliot Scheiner, Bill Schnee, Al Schmitt
Assistant Engineers: Lenise Bent, Ken Klinger, Linda Tyler, Ed
    Rack, Joe Bellamy, Ron Pangaliman

Executive Engineer: Roger Nichols
Mastered by: Bernie Grundman at A&M Studios, Hollywood

Recorded at: Village Recorders, West LA, Producer's Workshop, Hollywood, Warner Bros. North Hollywood Recording Studios, ABC Recording Studios, Sound Labs, Hollywood, A&R Studios, N.Y.C.

Bagman: Leonard Freedman
Production Coordinator: Barbara Miller
Covert Operations: Karen Stanley
Sound Consultant: Stuart Dawson
Hemiolas, Hockets, Maneries of Garlandia, etc.: Andrew Frank
Protection: Irving Azoff

Art Direction: Oz Studios
Designed by: Patricia Mitsui and Geoff Westen
Cover Photo: Hideki Fujii
Inside Photos: Walter Becker, Dorothy A. White

Black Cow

Drums: Paul Humphrey
Bass: Chuck Rainey
Electric Piano: Victor Feldman
Clavinet: Joe Sample
Guitar: Larry Carlton
Synthesizer: Donald Fagen
Tenor Sax: Tom Scott
Backing vocals: Clydie King, Venetta Fields, Sherlie Matthews, Rebecca Louis

Aja

Drums: Steve Gadd
Bass: Chuck Rainey
Guitars: Larry Carlton, Walter Becker, Denny Dias
Electric Piano: Joe Sample
Piano: Michael Omartian
Percussion: Victor Feldman
Synthesizers and Police Whistle: Donald Fagen
Tenor Sax: Wayne Shorter
Backing vocals: Donald Fagen, Tim Schmit

Deacon Blues

Drums: Bernard Purdie
Bass: Walter Becker
Guitars: Larry Carlton, Lee Ritenour
Electric Piano: Victor Feldman
Synthesizer: Donald Fagen
Tenor Sax: Pete Christlieb
Backing vocals: Clydie King, Sherlie Matthews, Venetta Fields

Peg

Drums: Rick Marotta
Bass: Chuck Rainey
Electric Piano: Paul Griffin
Clavinet: Don Grolnick
Guitar: Steve Khan
Solo Guitar: Jay Graydon
Percussion: Victor Feldman, Gary Coleman

Lyricon: Tom Scott
Backing vocals: Michael McDonald, Paul Griffin

Home at Last

Drums: Bernard Purdie
Bass: Chuck Rainey
Guitar: Larry Carlton
Solo Guitar: Walter Becker
Piano and Vibes: Victor Feldman
Synthesizer: Donald Fagen
Backing vocals: Donald Fagen, Tim Schmit

I Got the News

Drums: Ed Greene
Bass: Chuck Rainey
Piano, Vibes and Percussion: Victor Feldman
Guitar: Dean Parks
Solo Guitars: Walter Becker, Larry Carlton
Synthesizers: Donald Fagen
Backing vocals: Michael McDonald, Clydie King, Venetta Fields, Sherlie Matthews, Rebecca Louis

Josie

Drums: Jim Keltner
Bass: Chuck Rainey
Electric Piano: Victor Feldman
Guitars: Larry Carlton, Dean Parks
Solo Guitar: Walter Becker

Synthesizers: Donald Fagen
Persussion: Jim Keltner
Backing vocals: Donald Fagen, Tim Schmit

Steve Gadd and Michael McDonald appear through courtesy of Warner Bros. Records, Inc.
Chuck Rainey appears through courtesy of A&M Records, Inc.
Victor Feldman appears through courtesy of Caribou Records
Lee Ritenour appears through courtesy of Zembu Productions
Wayne Shorter appears through courtesy of Columbia Records, Inc.
Tom Scott appears through courtesy of Ode Records

Release Information / Chart History

ALBUM

Aja
ABC 1006
September 1977
US   #3
UK   #5
Canada   #3

SINGLES

"Peg" b/w "I Got the News"
ABC 12320
November 1977
US   #11
Canada   #7

"Deacon Blues" b/w "Home at Last"
ABC 12355
April 1978
US   #19
Canada   #14

"Josie" b/w "Black Cow"
ABC 12404
August 1978
US   #26
Canada   #20

* Aja *was also released on cassette and eight-track tape, and in limited gold and red vinyl editions. It was first reissued on CD in 1984. The 2000 remastered edition is recommended. None of* Aja's *singles charted in the UK.*

Selected Covers

"Black Cow"
Norman Connors / *Take It to the Limit* (Verve, 1980)
    feat. Venetta Fields, Freddie Hubbard
Ahmad Jamal / *One* (Verve, 1979)
    feat. Chuck Rainey, Hal Blaine

"Aja"
Christian McBride / *Sci-Fi* (MCA, 2000)
    feat. Herbie Hancock, David Gilmore
Various Artists / *The Royal Dan: A Tribute* (Tone Center, 2006)
    feat. Al Di Meola, Jimmy Haslip

"Deacon Blues"
Julian Coryell / *Duality* (Encoded, 1997)
    feat. Bob Mintzer, Billy Hart
Hoops McCann Band / *Plays the Music of Steely Dan* (MCA, 1988)
    feat. Chuck Findley, Paul Humphrey

"Peg"

Cornell Dupree / *Shadow Dancing* (Versatile, 1978)
    feat. Hank Crawford, Jimmy Smith
Mike Mandel / *Sky Music* (Vanguard, 1978)
    feat. David Sanborn, Lew Soloff

"Home at Last"

Rosanne Agasee / *Home at Last* (Ind., 2005)
    feat. Doug Riley, Jake Langley
Michael Paulo / *One Passion* (MCA, 1989)
    feat. Carlos Vega, Alex Acuña

"I Got the News"

Woody Herman Band / *Chick, Donald, Walter & Woodrow* (Century, 1978)
    feat. Tom Scott, Victor Feldman
Justin Morell / *The Music of Steely Dan* (Sonic Frenzy, 2002)
    feat. John Guerin, Tom Peterson

"Josie"

Larry Carlton / *On Solid Ground* (MCA, 1989)
    feat. Dean Parks, Rick Marotta
Steve Ferrone / *It Up* (Drumroll, 2003)
    feat. Joey DeFrancesco, Gerald Albright

Glossary

Aeolian. See "Modes."

Altered Tensions. Chord extensions drawn from the so-called "altered scale." The term usually refers to the use of exotic pitches—b9, #9, b5, b13—over dominant chords.

Anaphora. The repetition of a phrase at key intervals within a spoken or sung passage.

Arranger. As distinct from "composer." An arranger organizes, embellishes and creates separate parts for an existing composition; when the arranger is as accomplished as Tom Scott, his contribution constitutes an important part of the creative whole.

Art Song. Any of several varieties of serious vocal composition. Nineteenth-century French composer (and Donald Fagen influence) Gabriel Fauré was one of its best known exponents.

Assonance. Repeated vowel sounds embedded in a lyric, poem or prose passage; distinct from rhyme.

Bacharach, Burt. Popular songwriter who bridged the gap between the Great American Songbook era and the swinging sixties.

Becker and Fagen admired his use of cutting-edge harmony, unexpected key changes and odd meters.

Basie, Count. Swing-era pianist and bandleader who, along with contemporaries Duke Ellington and Louis Armstrong, oversaw jazz's first golden age.

Beat Poetry. Jazz-influenced verse originating in the fifties Beat scene in New York City. Allen Ginsberg's masterpiece "Howl" is the best known example; other Beat poets included Gregory Corso and and Gary Snyder.

Bebop. Jazz genre pioneered in the mid-forties by Charlie Parker, Dizzy Gillespie, Bud Powell and others. It broke the swing mold by focusing on streams of intricate, improvised melody by individual players.

Beiderbecke, Bix. Roaring-twenties jazz cornetist whose influence far exceeded his twenty-eight-year life span. His admirers included Louis Armstrong and Miles Davis.

Bland, Bobby. Hall-of-fame blues singer. Bobby "Blue" Bland's hits were more harmonically developed and subtly arranged than those of most bluesmen. His best known record is 1961's "I Pity the Fool."

Blue Note Records. Arguably the most important record label in the history of jazz. Founded in 1939 and currently an EMI imprint, it has over the years released recordings by almost every major figure in jazz, including Thelonius Monk, John Coltrane, Art Blakey, Herbie Hancock, Horace Silver, Dexter Gordon, Wayne Shorter, Clifford Brown, Kenny Burrell, Freddie Hubbard, Sonny Rollins, McCoy Tyner, Lee Morgan and Ornette Coleman.

Blues Form. Generally a twelve-bar pattern derived from the I-IV-I-V-IV-I structure of basic (i.e. non-jazz) blues. Because it is so entrenched in popular song, blues form remains recognizable even if altered substantially.

Bossa. Short for "bossa nova," the smooth Latin pop style that emerged from Brazil in the early sixties. The term now applies not just to indigenous Brazilian examples, but to any composition built on the rhythmic architecture of bossa nova.

Chandleresque. In the style of Raymond Chandler, the writer who immortalized swing-era Los Angeles.

Changes. Shorthand for "chord changes" or "chord progression."

Chart. Common slang for sheet music used at a gig or recording session.

Chord Nomenclature. In jazz, chords tend to be identified by their four "chord tones" (usually tonic, third, fifth and sixth or seventh), with extensions, or notes beyond the first octave, listed separately. Thus, "$C^{7(\#9)}$" is the tonic, third, fifth and flat seventh of C, with the sharp ninth degree (in this case a D#) added.

Chromatic. Moving in half steps. "Chromatic" can also describe the overall color of a piece that contains prominent chromatic melody notes or is built on chromatic harmony.

Clavinet. Basically an electric harpsichord. A core instrument in the funk arsenal, the clavinet can be heard on many Steely Dan tunes, including "Black Cow," "Kid Charlemagne," "Green Earrings" and "Night by Night."

Click Track. An audio track containing a metronomic pulse that orients players to a strict rhythmic grid (and to each other).

Coltrane, John. Even more than Lester Young and Sonny Rollins, 'Trane was the premier tenor saxophonist in jazz; he also rekindled interest in the soprano saxophone when he took it up in the late fifties. His career, like that of Miles Davis, spanned several movements, including bebop, modal jazz and free jazz.

Crusaders. Funk quartet led by keyboardist/composer (and *Aja/ Gaucho* sideman) Joe Sample. The Crusaders' distinctive, gritty sound amounted to a kind of instrumental soul.

Davis, Miles. Trumpeter, bandleader and composer whose influence was felt strongly in at least five phases of jazz, from bebop to fusion. His effect on jazz cannot be overstated; the music simply would not be recognizable without him. His most important albums include *Milestones, Kind of Blue, Sketches of Spain, In a Silent Way* and *Bitches Brew*.

Deconstruction. The loading of a text with secondary meanings or implicit conflicts that tend to cast doubt on the text's primary meaning; a postmodern species of irony.

Diatonic. Relating to, or not exceeding the boundaries of, a standard seven-note scale. Nondiatonic material, like the third chord in the chorus of "Black Cow"(a IV^{13sus4} in the key of A Major), tends to attract attention to itself.

Dissonance. Note combinations deemed unpleasant due to violations of harmonic/acoustic rules.

Dominant Function. The presence of both a major third and flattened seventh in a chord indicates the chord has dominant color. The chord has dominant *function* if resolves down a fifth (up a fourth) or down a semitone. The dominant chords in the intro of "Peg," for example, have dominant function because they resolve downward by half steps.

Dorian. See "Modes."

Downbeat. A strong rhythmic point corresponding either to the beginning of a piece or the beginning of a measure.

Dynamic Range. The ratio of the loudest sound in a track to the softest sound in a track.

Ellington, Duke. Iconic composer, bandleader and pianist.

Ellington's innovative compositions in the jazz realm drew on sources from around the world, and advanced the harmonic language of popular song by leaps and bounds. His best known songs include "Sophisticated Lady," "Prelude to a Kiss," "Cotton Tail" and—Dan fans take note—"East St. Louis Toodle-oo."

Evans, Bill. One of the most influential pianists in the history of jazz; also an accomplished composer. Evans appeared on *Kind of Blue*, but is best known for his own startling, lyrical recordings as a leader, as well as his distinctive, harmonically rich left-hand comping style. He wrote "Waltz for Debby," "Very Early" and "Peri's Scope."

Evans, Gil. Composer/arranger best known for his work with Miles Davis's large groups between 1957 and 1960.

George, Lowell. Founder and guiding spirit of Little Feat; died in 1979. Like Becker and Fagen, George made it his business to interweave various strands of American music (in his case, rock, country, folk, funk, bluegrass and soul).

Gordon, Dexter. Highly regarded tenor saxophonist with roots in bebop. Along with fellow expat Bud Powell, Gordon honed his playing style in Europe in the sixties. His way with a ballad, especially his distinctive backphrasing, is legendary.

Great American Songbook. Blanket term for the slew of popular standards that emerged from Broadway and Tin Pan Alley beginning in the twenties.

Groove. The interaction of the rhythmic components of an arrangement.

Harmony. The polyphonic (or "vertical") aspect of music. In pop and jazz, "harmony" is used interchangeably with "chord progression" or "changes."

Ionian. See "Modes."

Key Signature. A specific combination of notated sharps or flats that indicates the tonal center (and necessary accidentals) for a given passage of music.

Kind of Blue . 1959 Miles Davis album widely considered to be the most influential, not to mention popular, recording in the history of jazz. Also featuring John Coltrane and Bill Evans, *Kind of Blue* represents modal jazz's ground zero.

Leiber and Stoller. Jerry Leiber and Mike Stoller. One of the only rock-era songwriting teams to make serious use of the Tin Pan Alley model, the duo wrote hits for Charles Brown, Elvis Presley, the Coasters and the Drifters.

Loesser, Frank. Composer and lyricist best known for his 1950 musical *Guys and Dolls*. He had extraordinary facility weaving slang and modern idioms into popular song. Covered by Miles Davis, John Coltrane, Sonny Rollins, McCoy Tyner, many others.

Lydian. See "Modes."

Mandel, Johnny. Renowned composer/arranger specializing in film music. The former Count Basie arranger co-wrote the standards "The Shadow of Your Smile" and "Suicide Is Painless" (the theme from *M*A*S*H*).

Mastering. The preparation of recorded music for release. More than simply a media transfer, mastering gives producers and artists a final chance to tweak the overall sound of their mixes (though not the balance among the instruments).

McLean, Jackie. Jazz alto saxophonist whose collaborators included Miles Davis, Sonny Rollins, Charles Mingus, Art Blakey, Dexter Gordon and Freddie Hubbard.

Measure. Synonymous with "bar." Measures parse a composition into distinct, recurring chunks comprised of a specific number of beats.

Melody. Synonymous with "tune"; literally, the sequence of notes that constitutes the "lead" part of a piece of music, whether sung or played.

MIDI. Musical Instrument Digital Interface; a protocol that allows computers and music devices to function synchronously.

Mingus, Charles. Iconoclastic jazz composer, bandleader and bassist. His hard-bop recordings and quirky compositions continue to challenge today.

Mixed-Meter. Having more than one time signature. "Where Am I Going," the Gino Vannelli song referred to in the text, alternates between 5/4 and 4/4.

Mixolydian. See "Modes."

Modal Interpolation. The insertion of chords or melodic material from one mode into another. In "Josie," the Fmaj$^{9(no3)}$ in bar 24 is interpolated from the parallel Phrygian mode.

Modal Jazz. Jazz built on modal scales (see "Modes") as opposed to conventional chord progressions. Miles Davis's *Kind of Blue* was the flagship record of the movement. Because western ears are acclimatized to the Ionian (major) and Aeolian (minor) modes, most modal jazz is based on more exotic modes like the Myxolydian ("All Blues") or Dorian ("So What").

Modes. The Greek musical modes: Ionian, a major scale; Dorian, a minor scale with a raised sixth; Phrygian, a minor scale with a lowered second; Lydian, a major scale with a raised fourth; Mixolydian, a major scale with a lowered seventh; Aeolian, a minor scale; and the rarely heard (and highly unstable) Locrian, a minor scale with a lowered fifth and a lowered second. Popular awareness of modes increased substantially as a result of Miles Davis's modal and polymodal compositions on *Kind of Blue*.

Modulation. Synonymous with "key change." A modulation is a perceived shift from one tonal center to another.

Monk, Thelonius. Extraordinary jazz composer and pianist. Monk's angular playing style helped bebop morph into postbop. His best known compositions include "Straight, No Chaser," "'Round Midnight" and "Well, You Needn't."

Monophonic. Consisting of single notes. Early synthesizers (including the ubiquitous Minimoog) were monophonic because the technology required for polyphony was, at the time, dauntingly complex.

Multitracking. The process of recording more than one musical performance to separate tracks. When it involves adding parts to a preexisting piece, multitracking is called "overdubbing." Like all major-label releases of the day, *Aja* was multitracked to twenty-four-track, two-inch audio tape.

Muted Trumpet. Trumpets can accommodate several varieties of mute, but the "muted trumpet" sound most familiar to contemporary audiences is the thin, metallic "Harmon mute" tone popularized by Miles Davis.

NARAS. The National Academy of Recording Arts & Sciences. Comprised of music industry professionals, NARAS is the body that, since 1959, has presented the annual Grammy Awards. Steely Dan's 2000 comeback album *Two Against Nature* won four Grammys (including "Album of the Year") at the '01 ceremonies, indicating to some that the existence of a benevolent God was not entirely out of the question.

Nelson, Oliver. Jazz saxophonist and composer. Nelson's 1961 septet album *The Blues and the Abstract Truth*, featuring Bill Evans, Freddie Hubbard and Eric Dolphy, was a major influence on Steely Dan. Fagen has spoken approvingly of Nelson's sense of swing and his combining of jazz streams old and new.

Odysseus. The seafaring hero of *The Odyssey*. In the episode to which Becker and Fagen allude, Odysseus is lashed to the mast of his ship so he will not be tempted by the Sirens' (mermaids') song.

Ostinato. A repeated musical pattern; classical nomenclature for "vamp." Used in moderation, ostinati can create a pleasantly hypnotic effect.

Parker, Charlie. Also known as "Bird." Icon, innovator, band-leader, composer, bebop genius, lightspeed improviser, Dizzy Gillespie cohort, greatest-ever alto saxophonist, symbol of sub-stance-abuse tragedy.

Pastorius, Jaco. Meteoric electric bassist known for his recordings with Weather Report, Joni Mitchell and the Pat Metheny Group. Pastorius is one of a handful of musicians in the history of jazz who can be said to have single-handedly revolutionized his instrument. He died at thirty-five.

Pentatonic. Consisting of five notes. The core notes in a blues scale form a "minor pentatonic" scale.

Phrygian. See "Modes."

Porter, Cole. Sole author of the standards "Night and Day," "Love for Sale," "In the Still of the Night," "Easy to Love," "Every Time We Say Goodbye," "I Love Paris," "All of You," and many more; one of only a few Broadway greats who wrote both lyrics and music. His harmonically challenging, often melancholy tunes are considered core repertoire by jazz musicians.

Postbop. Eclectic sixties jazz style represented by Wayne Shorter, McCoy Tyner, Herbie Hancock, others.

Reich, Steve. Influential minimalist composer. Reich's work struc-turally resembles the work of Philip Glass, but, where Glass's tends to create a feeling of numbness and/or entrapment,

Reich's has exuberance and points of revelatory release.

Rhodes. The Fender Rhodes electric piano. Popularized by Chick Corea, Herbie Hancock, Joe Zawinul, Stevie Wonder and others, the Rhodes was integral to the Steely Dan sound. As Lee Ritenour points out, "the tunes were based around Donald Fagen's Rhodes parts." Fagen's distinctive Rhodes sound was achieved by sending the instrument's output through a pair of slow-sweeping MXR "Phase 90" phase shifter pedals.

Root. The tonic degree of a scale or key; the note on which the so-called "I chord" is built.

Runyonesque. In the style of Damon Runyon, the writer who immortalized Prohibition-era New York.

Scale Degree. The designation of a note based on its distance from a tonic point, or point of rest, in a given key. The "sixth" in the key of C Major, for example, is A; the ninth is D; and so on.

Semitone, Half Step. A minor second interval. The musical distance represented by moving up or down one note (one adjacent key) on a piano.

Sequencer. A MIDI-controlled device that orders and reproduces electronic musical performances with precision. Sequencers gave eighties pop its double-Advil, clockwork thump; Fagen used them on record only in combination with real instruments ("New Frontier" is a good example).

Sisyphean. Destined to be foiled, again and again, by fate. In Greek mythology, Sisyphus was condemned by Zeus to roll a boulder up a steep hill for eternity; each time he neared the top, the rock rolled down, and he was forced to begin again.

Sonata Form. An eighteenth-century recipe for instrumental music. Its influence cannot be overstated. Specifying an order of events, a sequence of tonal centers and a particular species of development, it has proved useful to everyone from Mozart to present-day composers.

Swing. Shorthand for "the big-band era." Bebop's immediate antecedent, swing emphasized ensemble playing and danceable midtempo rhythms. Key figures included Duke Ellington, Count Basie, Artie Shaw, Benny Goodman, Woody Herman, Stan Kenton and the Dorsey brothers.

Syncopation. The stressing of what would normally be unstressed beats. A good example from *Aja* is the dotted-eighth rhythm of the phrase "big black cow": it begins on a downbeat but ends halfway between beat two and beat three.

Tag. Especially in jazz, the final section of a piece. A tag usually involves a repeated figure being enlivened by improvisation or variation. In pop, a tag often fades.

Tatum, Art. Mind-boggling pianist of the swing and early bebop era. Tatum was influential because of his unflinching individuality, sheer virtuosity and innovative reharmonizations of popular standards. He frequently recorded without accompaniment.

Tonal Center. Literally the key of a song or given section of a song. When "Black Cow" modulates from C Major to A Major, it can be said to have moved to a new tonal center.

Tone Poem. A single-movement orchestral piece that draws its inspiration from literature, mythology, visual art or other non-musical source. The impressionist composer Claude Debussy was among its chief exponents.

Tracking Date. In pop parlance, the recording session at which the "beds," or basic tracks, are laid down; as distinct from an "overdub" session (for horns, vocals, etc.).

Transition Chord. A chord that facilitates movement from one strong chord to another, or, often, one key to another.

Triad. A three-note chord, the sound of which is considered "square" in a jazz context. On their first few albums, Becker and Fagen relieved triad tedium by routinely including a ninth (or second) in their major chords; this was their much-discussed "Mu" major chord. After 1975, their harmonic palette expanded to include standard jazz harmony (see "Chord Nomencla-ture").

Tutti. Italian for "all." In a tutti section of music, the entire ensemble, or band, plays identical material.

Vamp. A repeated instrumental figure that signals a point of rest in an arrangement or provides accompaniment for improvisation; most common in jazz and R&B.

Verisimilitude. In the arts, authenticity or uncomplicated realism.

Voicing. The manner in which a chord is "stacked"; the color produced by a chord by virtue of the order of intervals in it. Starting with *Aja*, Becker and Fagen began to show a strong preference for "open" (postbop) voicings—stacks that emphasize seconds, fourths and fifths—in both their rhythm arrangements and horn arrangements.

Whole Tone, Whole Step. A major second interval. The musical distance represented by moving up or down two notes (adjacent keys) on a piano.

Woods, Phil. King of post-Parker alto saxophone. His excursions into the pop world include Steely Dan's "Doctor Wu," Billy Joel's "Just the Way You Are" and Paul Simon's "Have a Good Time."

Yellowjackets. Grammy-winning West Coast instrumental quartet; equal parts jazz, funk and Brazilian. The title track of their 1986 album *Shades* was written by Donald Fagen.

Young, Lester. Swing-era tenor player whose influence on subsequent generations of saxophonists was profound. Young is the subject of the jazz standards "Lester Leaps In," "Lester Left

Town" and "Goodbye Pork Pie Hat."

Zawinul, Joe. Fusion progenitor, keyboardist, composer. After helping Miles Davis invent what was then called "jazz rock," Zawinul founded Weather Report and became a mentor to a twenty-four-year-old bass player from Florida named Jaco Pastorius. His best known composition is the 1977 Weather Report crossover hit "Birdland."

Recommended Listening

Mose Allison
Mose Allison Sings (Prestige, 1957)
The Band
Music from Big Pink (Capitol, 1968)
Count Basie
Lil' Ol' Groovemaker (Verve, 1962)
The Beatles
Revolver (Parlophone, 1966)
Jeff Beck
Wired (Epic, 1976)
Walter Becker
11 Tracks of Whack (Giant, 1994)
Art Blakey & the Jazz Messengers
Moanin' (Blue Note, 1958)
Bobby Bland
Two Steps from the Blues (Duke, 1961)
The Brecker Brothers
Straphangin' (Arista, 1981)

Clifford Brown / Max Roach
    Clifford Brown & Max Roach (EmArcy, 1954)
Kenny Burrell
    Midnight Blue (Blue Note, 1963)
Larry Carlton
    Last Nite (MCA, 1986)
Ray Charles
    The Genius of Ray Charles (Atlantic, 1959)
    Genius+Soul=Jazz (Impulse, 1961)
    Modern Sounds in Country and Western Music (ABC, 1962)
Chicago
    Chicago V (Columbia, 1972)
Pete Christlieb / Warne Marsh
    Apogee (Warner Bros., 1978)
John Coltrane
    Blue Train (Blue Note, 1957)
    Giant Steps (Atlantic, 1960)
    A Love Supreme (Impulse, 1964)
Ry Cooder
    Bop Till You Drop (Warner Bros., 1979)
Chick Corea
    Three Quartets (Warner Bros., 1981)
The Crusaders
    Those Southern Knights (Blue Thumb, 1976)
    Free as the Wind (Blue Thumb, 1977)
Miles Davis
    Birth of the Cool (Capitol, 1957)
    Kind of Blue (Columbia, 1959)
    Sketches of Spain (Columbia, 1960)
    In a Silent Way (Columbia, 1969)

Deodato
   Prelude (CTI, 1973)
Bob Dylan
   Highway 61 Revisited (Columbia, 1965)
   Blonde on Blonde (Columbia, 1966)
Duke Ellington / John Coltrane
   Duke Ellington & John Coltrane (Impulse, 1962)
The Don Ellis Orchestra
   Electric Bath (Columbia, 1967)
Bill Evans
   Sunday at the Village Vanguard (Riverside, 1961)
   Conversations with Myself (Verve, 1963)
   Montreux II (CTI, 1970)
   Affinity (Warner Bros., 1978)
   We Will Meet Again (Warner Bros., 1979)
Donald Fagen
   The Nightfly (Warner Bros., 1982)
   Kamakiriad (Reprise, 1993)
   Morph the Cat (Warner Bros., 2006)
Aretha Franklin
   Young, Gifted and Black (Atlantic, 1971)
Michael Franks
   Sleeping Gypsy (Warner Bros., 1977)
Marvin Gaye
   What's Going On (Tamla, 1971)
Stan Getz / Bill Evans
   Stan Getz & Bill Evans (Verve, 1964)
Dexter Gordon
   Go (Blue Note, 1962)

Herbie Hancock
Maiden Voyage (Blue Note, 1965)
Head Hunters (Columbia, 1973)
Woody Herman
Chick, Donald, Walter & Woodrow (Century, 1978)
Freddie Hubbard
Red Clay (CTI, 1970)
Al Jarreau
Breakin' Away (Warner Bros., 1981)
Rickie Lee Jones
Rickie Lee Jones (Warner Bros., 1979)
Pirates (Warner Bros., 1981)
Wynton Kelly / Wes Mongomery
Smokin' at the Half Note (Verve, 1965)
Stan Kenton
New Concepts of Artistry in Rhythm (Capitol, 1953)
Steve Khan / Rob Mounsey
Local Color (Denon, 1987)
Little Feat
Dixie Chicken (Warner Bros., 1973)
Time Loves a Hero (Warner Bros., 1977)
Curtis Mayfield
Curtis (Curtom, 1970)
Jackie McLean
Let Freedom Ring (Blue Note, 1962)
Harold Melvin & the Blue Notes
Wake Up Everybody (Philadelphia International, 1975)
The Meters
Rejuvenation (Reprise, 1974)

Charles Mingus
  Mingus Ah Um (Columbia, 1959)
Joni Mitchell
  Court and Spark (Asylum, 1974)
  Hejira (Asylum, 1976)
Thelonius Monk
  Monk's Dream (Columbia, 1963)
Lee Morgan
  The Sidewinder (Blue Note, 1963)
Oliver Nelson
  The Blues and the Abstract Truth (Impulse, 1961)
Randy Newman
  Little Criminals (Warner Bros., 1977)
The O'Jays
  Back Stabbers (Philadelphia International, 1972)
Junior Parker
  Love Ain't Nothin' But a Business Goin' On (Groove Merchant, 1971)
Steve Reich
  Variations for Winds, Strings and Keyboards (Philips, 1983)
Lee Ritenour
  Captain Fingers (Epic, 1977)
Sonny Rollins
  Saxophone Colossus (Prestige, 1956)
Todd Rundgren
  Something/Anything? (Bearsville, 1972)
Leon Russell
  Carney (Shelter, 1972)
David Sanborn
  As We Speak (Warner Bros., 1982)

Boz Scaggs
   Silk Degrees (Columbia, 1976)
Wayne Shorter
   See No Evil (Blue Note, 1965)
Horace Silver
   Song for My Father (Blue Note, 1964)
Paul Simon
   Still Crazy After All These Years (Columbia, 1975)
   One-Trick Pony (Warner Bros., 1980)
Dusty Springfield
   Dusty in Memphis (Atlantic, 1969)
Steely Dan
   Can't Buy a Thrill (ABC, 1972)
   Countdown to Ecstasy (ABC, 1973)
   Pretzel Logic (ABC, 1974)
   Katy Lied (ABC, 1975)
   The Royal Scam (ABC, 1976)
   Gaucho (MCA, 1980)
   Alive in America (Giant, 1995)
   Two Against Nature (Giant, 2000)
   Everything Must Go (Reprise, 2003)
Steps Ahead
   Steps Ahead (Elektra Musician, 1983)
   Modern Times (Elektra Musician, 1984)
The Stylistics
   Round 2 (Avco, 1972)
Traffic
   The Low Spark of High Heeled Boys (Island, 1971)
McCoy Tyner
   The Real McCoy (Blue Note, 1967)

Tom Waits
    Rain Dogs (Island, 1985)
War
    The World Is a Ghetto (UA, 1972)
Weather Report
    Heavy Weather (Columbia, 1977)
    Mr. Gone (Columbia, 1978)
Stevie Wonder
    Talking Book (Tamla, 1972)
    Innervisions (Tamla, 1973)
    Fulfillingness' First Finale (Tamla, 1974)
    Songs in the Key of Life (Motown, 1976)
Phil Woods
    Live from the Showboat (RCA, 1977)
Yellowjackets
    Yellowjackets (Warner Bros., 1981)
    Mirage a Trois (Warner Bros., 1983)

Bibliography

Bangs, Lester. *Psychotic Reactions and Carburetor Dung.* New York: Alfred A. Knopf, 1988.

Christgau, Robert. *Rock Albums of the '70s: A Critical Guide.* New Haven: Ticknor & Fields, 1981.

Feather, Leonard & Ira Gitler. *The Encyclopedia of Jazz in the '70s.* New York: Horizon Press, 1976.

Flanagan, Bill. *Written in My Soul: Rock's Great Songwriters Talk About Creating Their Music.* Chicago: Contemporary Books, 1986.

Friedwald, Will. *Stardust Melodies: The Biography of Twelve of America's Most popular Songs.* New York: Random House, 2002.

Gelmis, Joseph. *The Film Director as Superstar.* New York: Doubleday, 1970.

Hornby, Nick. *Songbook.* New York: Riverhead, 2003.

Johnstone, Nick. *The Melody Maker History of 20th Century Popular Music.* London: Bloomsbury, 1999.

Klosterman, Chuck. *Sex, Drugs, and Cocoa Puffs: A Low Culture Manifesto.* New York: Scribner, 2003.

Larkin, Colin, ed. *The Virgin Encyclopedia of Seventies Music.* London: Virgin Books, 1997.

McLuhan, Marshall. *Understanding Media.* Toronto: McGraw-Hill, 1964.

Milkowski, Bill. *Jaco: The Extraordinary and Tragic Life of Jaco Pastorius.* San Francisco: Miller Freeman Books, 1995.

Nisenson, Eric. *The Making of Kind of Blue: Miles Davis and His Masterpiece.* New York: St. Martin's, 2000.

Stokes, Geoffrey. *Starmaking Machinery: The Odyssey of an Album.* Indianapolis: Bobbs-Merrill, 1976.

Strong, Martin C., ed. *The Great Rock Discography.* Edinburgh: Mojo Books, 1994.

Sweet, Brian. *Steely Dan: Reelin' in the Years.* London: Omnibus Press, 1994.

Wadhams, Wayne. *Inside the Hits: The Seduction of a Rock and Roll Generation.* Boston: Berklee Press, 2001.

Wilder, Alec. *American Popular Song: The Great Innovators, 1900–1950.* New York: Oxford University Press, 1972.

Williams, Paul. *The 20th Century's Greatest Hits: A Top 40 List.* New York: Forge, 2000.

I've also gleaned many a steely tidbit from these magazines and newspapers over the years: *Rolling Stone, Down Beat, Billboard, Musician, Metal Leg, Jazziz, Mojo, Q, Paste, Melody Maker, New Musical Express, Goldmine, Creem, Crawdaddy!, Mix, Keyboard, Modern Drummer,* the *Village Voice.*

Also available in the series

1. *Dusty in Memphis* by Warren Zanes
2. *Forever Changes* by Andrew Hultkrans
3. *Harvest* by Sam Inglis
4. *The Kinks Are the Village Green Preservation Society* by Andy Miller
5. *Meat Is Murder* by Joe Pernice
6. *The Piper at the Gates of Dawn* by John Cavanagh
7. *Abba Gold* by Elisabeth Vincentelli
8. *Electric Ladyland* by John Perry
9. *Unknown Pleasures* by Chris Ott
10. *Sign 'O' the Times* by Michaelangelo Matos
11. *The Velvet Underground and Nico* by Joe Harvard
12. *Let It Be* by Steve Matteo
13. *Live at the Apollo* by Douglas Wolk
14. *Aqualung* by Allan Moore
15. *OK Computer* by Dai Griffiths
16. *Let It Be* by Colin Meloy
17. *Led Zeppelin IV* by Erik Davis
18. *Exile on Main Street* by Bill Janovitz
19. *Pet Sounds* by Jim Fusilli
20. *Ramones* by Nicholas Rombes
21. *Armed Forces* by Franklin Bruno
22. *Murmur* by J. Niimi
23. *Grace* by Daphne Brooks
24. *Endtroducing . . .* by Eliot Wilder
25. *Kick Out the Jams* by Don McLeese
26. *Low* by Hugo Wilcken
27. *Born in the U.S.A.* by Geoffrey Himes
28. *Music from Big Pink* by John Niven
29. *In the Aeroplane Over the Sea* by Kim Cooper
30. *Paul's Boutique* by Dan LeRoy
31. *Doolittle* by Ben Sisario
32. *There's a Riot Goin' On* by Miles Marshall Lewis
33. *The Stone Roses* by Alex Green
34. *In Utero* by Gillian G. Gaar
35. *Highway 61 Revisited* by Mark Polizzotti
36. *Loveless* by Mike McGonigal
37. *The Who Sell Out* by John Dougan
38. *Bee Thousand* by Marc Woodworth
39. *Daydream Nation* by Matthew Stearns
40. *Court and Spark* by Sean Nelson
41. *Use Your Illusion Vols 1 and 2* by Eric Weisbard
42. *Songs in the Key of Life* by Zeth Lundy
43. *The Notorious Byrd Brothers* by Ric Menck

44. *Trout Mask Replica* by Kevin Courrier
45. *Double Nickels on the Dime* by Michael T. Fournier
46. *Aja* by Don Breithaupt
47. *People's Instinctive Travels and the Paths of Rhythm* by Shawn Taylor
48. *Rid of Me* by Kate Schatz
49. *Achtung Baby* by Stephen Catanzarite
50. *If You're Feeling Sinister* by Scott Plagenhoef
51. *Pink Moon* by Amanda Petrusich
52. *Let's Talk About Love* by Carl Wilson
53. *Swordfishtrombones* by David Smay
54. *20 Jazz Funk Greats* by Drew Daniel
55. *Horses* by Philip Shaw
56. *Master of Reality* by John Darnielle
57. *Reign in Blood* by D. X. Ferris
58. *Shoot Out the Lights* by Hayden Childs
59. *Gentlemen* by Bob Gendron
60. *Rum, Sodomy & the Lash* by Jeffery T. Roesgen
61. *The Gilded Palace of Sin* by Bob Proehl
62. *Pink Flag* by Wilson Neate
63. *XO* by Matthew LeMay
64. *Illmatic* by Matthew Gasteier
65. *Radio City* by Bruce Eaton
66. *One Step Beyond . . .* by Terry Edwards
67. *Another Green World* by Geeta Dayal
68. *Zaireeka* by Mark Richardson
69. *69 Love Songs* by L. D. Beghtol
70. *Facing Future* by Dan Kois
71. *It Takes a Nation of Millions to Hold Us Back* by Christopher R. Weingarten
72. *Wowee Zowee* by Bryan Charles
73. *Highway to Hell* by Joe Bonomo
74. *Song Cycle* by Richard Henderson
75. *Spiderland* by Scott Tennent
76. *Kid A* by Marvin Lin
77. *Tusk* by Rob Trucks
78. *Pretty Hate Machine* by Daphne Carr
79. *Chocolate and Cheese* by Hank Shteamer
80. *American Recordings* by Tony Tost
81. *Some Girls* by Cyrus Patell
82. *You're Living All Over Me* by Nick Attfield
83. *Marquee Moon* by Bryan Waterman
84. *Amazing Grace* by Aaron Cohen
85. *Dummy* by R. J. Wheaton
86. *Fear of Music* by Jonathan Lethem
87. *Histoire de Melody Nelson* by Darran Anderson
88. *Flood* by S. Alexander Reed and Elizabeth Sandifer

89. *I Get Wet* by Phillip Crandall

90. *Selected Ambient Works Volume II* by Marc Weidenbaum

91. *Entertainment!* by Kevin J.H. Dettmar

92. *Blank Generation* by Pete Astor

93. *Donuts* by Jordan Ferguson

94. *Smile* by Luis Sanchez

95. *Definitely Maybe* by Alex Niven

96. *Exile in Guyville* by Gina Arnold

97. *My Beautiful Dark Twisted Fantasy* by Kirk Walker Graves

98. *The Grey Album* by Charles Fairchild

99. *( )* by Ethan Hayden

100. *Dangerous* by Susan Fast

101. *Tago Mago* by Alan Warner

102. *Ode to Billie Joe* by Tara Murtha

103. *Live Through This* by Anwen Crawford

104. *Freedom of Choice* by Evie Nagy

105. *Fresh Fruit for Rotting Vegetables* by Michael Stewart Foley

106. *Super Mario Bros.* by Andrew Schartmann

107. *Beat Happening* by Bryan C. Parker

108. *Metallica* by David Masciotra

109. *A Live One* by Walter Holland

110. *Bitches Brew* by George Grella Jr.

111. *Parallel Lines* by Kembrew McLeod

112. *Workingman's Dead* by Buzz Poole

113. *Hangin' Tough* by Rebecca Wallwork

114. *Geto Boys* by Rolf Potts

115. *Sleater-Kinney's Dig Me Out* by Jovana Babovic

116. *LCD Soundsystem's Sound of Silver* by Ryan Leas

117. *Donny Hathaway's Donny Hathaway Live* by Emily J. Lordi

118. *The Jesus and Mary Chain's Psychocandy* by Paula Mejia

119. *The Modern Lovers' The Modern Lovers* by Sean L. Maloney

120. *Angelo Badalamenti's Soundtrack from Twin Peaks* by Clare Nina Norelli

121. *Young Marble Giants' Colossal Youth* by Michael Blair and Joe Bucciero

122. *The Pharcyde's Bizarre Ride II the Pharcyde* by Andrew Barker

123. *The Suburbs* by Eric Eidelstein

124. *Workbook* by Walter Biggins and Daniel Couch

125. *Uptown Saturday Night* by Sean L. Maloney

126. *The Raincoats* by Jenn Pelly

127. *Homogenic* by Emily Mackay

128. *Okie* from Muskogee by Rachel Lee Rubin

129. *In on the Kill Taker* by Joe Gross

130. *24 Hour Revenge Therapy* by Ronen Givony

131. *Transformer* by Ezra Furman